OPEN ROAD

This work is based in truth, but for reasons of rhetoric and privacy,
myriad details have been changed.

Direct all inquiries to:
info@hwy61press.org

Designed by Susan Wasinger
Printed in the United States

ISBN-13: 978-0-9824425-4-8
ISBN-10: 0-9824425-4-8

OPEN ROAD

Notes on the wild & woolly journey
of the 20-somethings—money included

MARK BUTLER

Hwy 61 Press

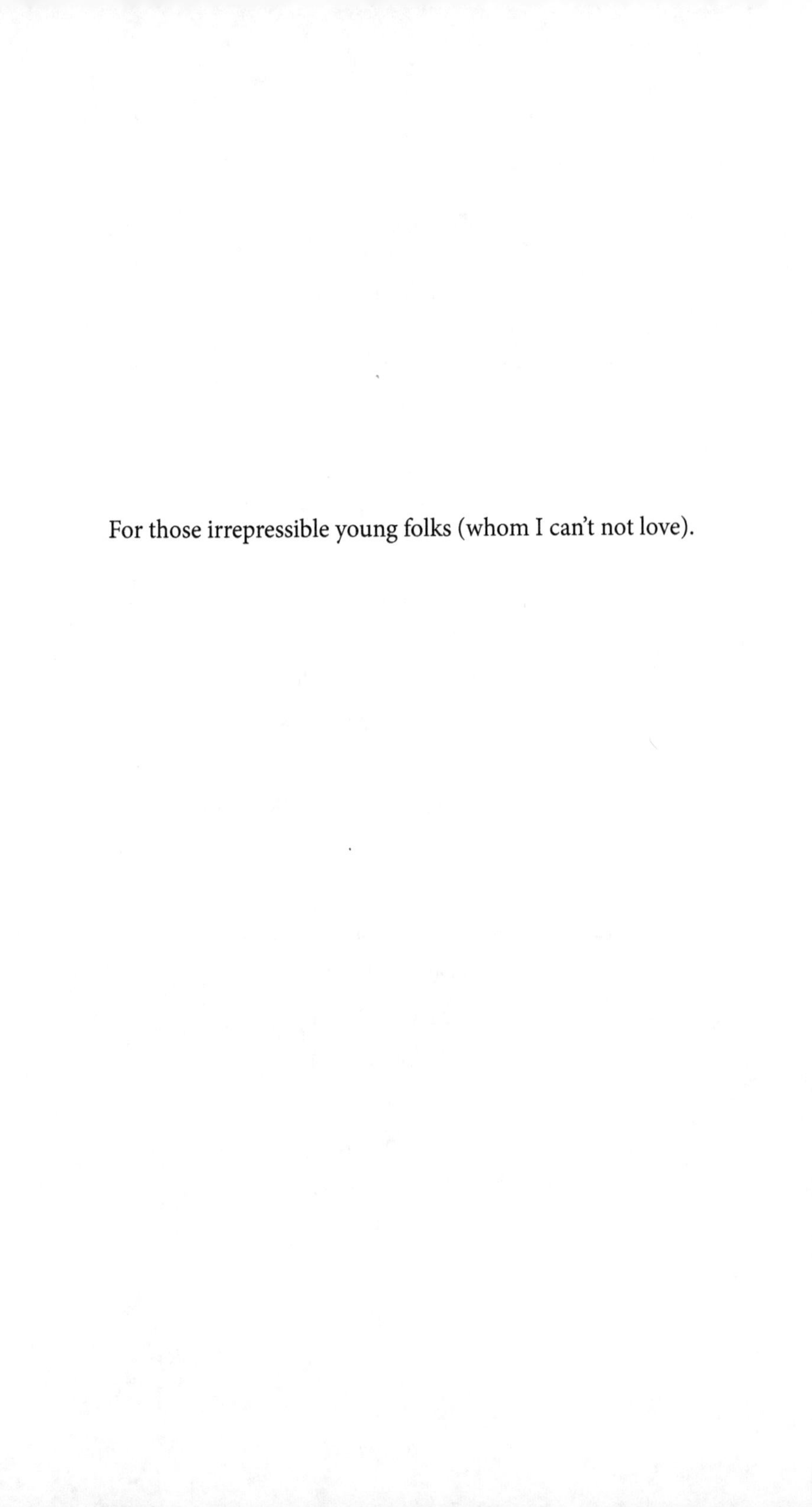

For those irrepressible young folks (whom I can't not love).

Mid-Amble

Amble On

Allons! Whoever you are, come travel with me!

Traveling with me you find what never tires.

The earth never tires,

The earth is rude, silent, incomprehensible at first, Nature is rude

and incomprehensible at first,

Be not discouraged, keep on, there are divine things enveloped,

I swear to you there are divine things more beautiful than words

can tell.

— WALT WHITMAN

PREAMBLE

Of course, we won't actually accompany our twenty-some-thing kids on their journey of the open road, no matter how soaring Whitman's poetry might make us feel. That would be silly. But like Merlin, Gandalf, Galadriel, and, well, yes, at times even like old JP Morgan, we all have our part to play in the great epic poem. What falls to us as parents seems doable, though it can be a bit dizzying. On any given day our role can instantaneously morph from parent to banker to friend to ticked off parent back to friend and—count on it!—back to banker. You're with me, right? There's more. Not all is flux. Behind the scenes of this morpharama is something quite unchanging. **We are serving as guide and educator to our kids, as intensely now as ever before.** Perhaps we saw this coming, perhaps not. But here it is now, and it's where our inquiry begins. Our main role in the great epic song is to somehow serve as impeccable guide to our twenty-some-thing kids. Some days that will be easier to do than others. No matter. Let's make a study of what's going on. Let's further the conversation, to wit, the one that will run like the bulls of Pamplona through our home life and through much, if not all, of this young-adult life corridor of our kids, say, ages 20 to 34.

This is a guidebook for the guides. And, whether we're guiding our own kid, our friend's kid, our niece, nephew, god-child—it matters not; the emotions have a way of running high with this love, life & money stuff. Entanglements extend as far as the eye can see. So, this too is a book of sorting, in which I at least hope to bring much needed sunlight and air to the ideas and trouble spots. On a practical note, I don't think it matters where you prefer to begin this work. Part One can be read second, or first. If you choose my ordering of things, you will find yourself forthwith in cartography mode, roaming and taking stock of the *territory*. What does it mean to come of age in early 21st-century America? What are the tasks that, on the open road of life, await most all young people from middle-/upper-middle class fami-lies? (No elitism intended here—just necessarily reporting from my own laboratory.) This is an essay about exploring the world and oneself, and how money curiously and consistently figures in. Put in the least sexy terms I can think of: I'm concerned with the economics of selfhood. Yes, I know, in such a short period of time, how far down have I taken us from Whitman and his poetic exhortations—well, stay tuned, I'm just getting started!

If you choose your ordering of things, that's also fine. Per-haps you're in no mood for what might feel like wisdom sight-seeing. Maybe you're already in the thick of it with your kid, and, right now, you'd like to dig in—to get on the right side of ABC teachings about saving, spending, planning, implementing, and so on. If so, go straight to Part Two. But fair warning: You'll still have to deal with Mark Butler's moderately weird Alterna-tive Money Universe and that means a little upfront effort will be required from you. Effort as in sticking with me while I weave thoughts on the four personal money Types *with* thoughts on the six competencies of personal finance *while* I bake a maple walnut pie and serve it with creamy vanilla ice cream. Okay, just joking about the pie and ice cream, but overall I think the effort put forth on learning the other stuff (psychological Types + personal finance Competencies) should pretty quickly save you both time and money. It won't hurt the relationship with your kid, either.

By the by, the four personal money Types aren't queued up so as to become yet another new set of beliefs that you have to buy. Rather, my interest is to get you thinking critically about how your kid ticks in this domain of personal money. I want all of us to work from that place. Vet your young person's strengths and weaknesses, and educate accordingly. Figure out how to bring to the fore his/her strengths, how to help him/her manage the weaknesses. Self-awareness is a genuine achievement when acting in this domain, and it is brought to completion by another psyche-based achievement, that of self-management. Working within this alternate framework, understanding what the targets are, clarifying outer tasks from psychological styles; now our words will have the best possible chance of resonating with our kids. I think that's all we can ask for.

So, begin with whichever part feels best.

. . . .

Before the gates officially fly open and we head for whatever hills suit us, I'd like to share a word on the spirit of this offering. In these matters of guiding the young people as they come of age, I am no expert. I have not made it to the Promised Land. And in case you suspect me of putting out some lame brand of false humility, I know you'll think differently when I recount how my twenty-something daughter hilariously (okay, hilariously now!) kicked my butt, and made my training as a family therapist and investment adviser and my experience as a semi-decent parent look woefully inadequate. There's more to the story, mostly of the feel good variety, though not all. Anyway, this is my moment to acknowledge the humanity of what's at play here. If we're good and we do the work, we'll get some victories, some defeats, and a whole lot of tie games. That's okay. It's the thing about learning and growing. We learn and grow. They learn and grow. And as for myself, the same ethos applies. The road goes on forever, and my life—*especially* in the areas where I feel a strong sense of mastery—remains a delightful and edgy work in progress. So you will find no reports herein from the Promised Land, much as that'd be a great story and doubtless sell lots of books.

Oh, and one final, not-so-small matter of a debt: Everywhere in this work I rip off Whitman. I steal his words and hang them all over the place as if they were my paintings. I play his songs on the turntable and act as if they came from my record collection. The reason for this shameless borrowing is twofold. One, the words are gorgeous. Bumping into beauty in the middle of an essay on money is never wrong. And, two, such words belong in a work like this. They make it responsible. They remind us of the view. They remind us of the ordinary and extraordinary nature of the journey. Anyway, I feel a sincere debt of gratitude to the Great American Bard, and, to make at least partial amends, I will send a little financial love to none other than Naropa University's Jack Kerouac School of Disembodied Poetics. Feels like the absolute least I can do.

Cheerful reading.
— MB

PART I

OPEN ROAD

Chapter 1 **Allons!**

Taking to the Open Road is its own beautiful and daring thing. Becoming your own person in this world takes tremendous moxie and skill and luck, along with a little help from your friends and family. At first blush these matters of emerging selfhood easily dwarf matters of money. For, who among us doesn't want our coming-of-age daughter to shine her light, to be her own person? Who doesn't wish our twenty-something son to kick it out, to pursue his own authentic path? Their victories delight us. Their defeats hit us like body blows. Many of us would pay most any sum to the gods to ensure that this decade of the twenties turns out well for the young people. In my book, this depth of emotion is healthy and good. It feels indicative of a kind of *relationship richness* in family life that prevails today, perhaps like never before. Even so, more is required. Depth of love needs its counterpoints and counterweights, at least in regards to the journey before us; that is, how we might educate the young people (ages 20 to 34) in the subtle and practical arts of money and personal finance.

For starters, I propose we ditch the usual financial tropes—

the ones that obsess about acquiring more money or winning the financial game (whatever that means). At the same time, I must say I dig the earthy side of money. Its weight, like gravity, is trustworthy. It invites us to be realistic, to be honest about who we are, and to really be in this world. The world has terms and money is a part of it. And while depth of love might impel us to do anything for our children, money shrewdly imposes limits. Each young person must become his or her own person, and financial self-reliance is part and parcel of this *separation/individuation* equation. Besides, let us speak freely among ourselves: No matter the socioeconomic niche we inhabit, our pockets only go so deep; indeed, our resources are finite, and dare I say, precious. We really do need the young people to progress along the path with all this money stuff.

GDIs & Bodhisattvas

I'm especially interested in what's at play for the twenty-something kids who choose to step off the beaten path. For them, I believe there's a kind of Henry David Thoreau-type dictum that applies: *The freer the spirit that a young person possesses, the more critical a solid financial education is for him/her.* But not any old sort of education will do. Indeed, that is what this work is devoted to exploring. How might we prepare the budding bodhisattva to skillfully navigate the capital side of life? How might we educate the irrepressible GDI (goddamn independent) who has ideas, millions of them, some reasonable and some very unreasonable? And, as for the artist and the poet and world traveler, or for that matter the rounded young person who inclines toward business or entrepreneurship or a trade or profession, with strong emphasis on the being rounded part—how might we educate him or her in matters of money? Now I am no cultural anthropologist, but surely we can agree that in 21st-century America it is matters of psyche and spirit that increasingly fuel the coming-of-age journey. This is a good thing. For, we cannot expect our kids to become great bodhisattvas in this world if they don't know who they are and what they're about.

But it mustn't stop there. This education can be no retread of the Follow-Your-Bliss ditty. While in some cultural quarters that advice has been a perennial, such sweet words are perilous for what they omit. Granted, the follow-your-bliss motto may help an otherwise inwardly-stuck young person to pick a life direction to explore; but, to say that everything will work itself out after that would be a great disservice. Practical skills need gathering. What is the plan? Is there a budget? Has it been looked at lately? What is the savings goal? Any progress on that front? Mental toughness also needs mustering. Fall down, get up, figure out the lesson to be learned. Repeat! And, last but not least, there is the matter of gathering a variety of data points on the lay of the capital land. This, too, is critical. How much should a gig like that pay? Where are the career ditches and dead ends in any given line of work? Who (such as a potential future boss) acts all groovy at the beginning of the relationship, but is an obnoxious creep and should be avoided at all costs? What kind of chops do I need, and what does it cost to become a __________, i.e., midwife, graphic designer, coffee roaster, web dude, techie, entrepreneur, lawyer, builder, handyman, investment adviser, etc.? When does it make sense to abandon a particular pursuit and go in a fresh direction?

Without putting some of these "provisions" in the proverbial backpack, and without the periodic restocking of such supplies, our kid will encounter more than his or her fair share of obstacles out there. To be clear, I'm not against mistakes. They're part of the journey. But some mistakes are much better, much more fertile and generative, than others. Which brings me to comment on an irony; one, I know, we can all live without. That is: We cannot expect the young people to develop their talents, to give their gifts, to shine their light—in short, to bring the planet back into balance one small act at a time, if they're constantly distracted and injured by the capital world we all live in. I'm on a mission to undermine this irony.

ANTHEM

The journey of the open road belongs to the young people; that is only right. At the same time, here we are. In relationship terms we find ourselves constantly and fluidly moving from one role to the next—now parent, next counselor, then us opening the wallet and serving as banker, then us closing the wallet and throwing a dark look, and now again visiting with them as great friends do. This morphing of roles is constant, and ordinary. Same is true for the myriad financial dealings and transactions that transpire between the young people and us. Indeed, this fact of family life can extend far into the decade of twenty-something life. And this is the opportunity. We're in the ideal position to educate them on an array of essential matters—matters that frequently have a financial component. Put differently, we're in the ideal position to talk with our kids about life, and help them integrate matters of money into that. Always, we listen first to their great spirit. Then we connect with the earth and think with them into the economic side of any given equation.

Panning back, I am aware that our country, our world, and the planet are under tremendous duress. Tremendous. At the same time, I unflinchingly believe in the possibilities of the future. This is synonymous with believing in the heart and talent of the emerging generation of young people in America. (I'm not excluding the young people around the world; I just don't profess to have a feel for where they're at.) I therefore think our investment of time and energy (and money) in the kids belongs on the short list of what is most important and timely in this life. I doubt I need to win you to this point of view, only to underscore here that the personal is the political. Nurturing young people to their spiritual-and-worldly fullness augurs well. Being authentic matters. Being savvy in the ways and means of the capital world matters. Our young people are the wealth of our great nation. Let us test them, educate them, support them, and in so doing let them go—so they can go deep into the future.

Allons! The inducements will be greater,

We will sail pathless and wild seas,

We will go where winds blow, waves dash, and the Yankee clipper

speeds by under full sail.

— Walt Whitman

Chapter 2 **Mark's Song**

For starters, yes, it is true, I was once a tiny pumpkin growing on a pumpkin vine ...

You want photos? You want stories? You want to know what I was up to back in the day?

Understood.

You want to know about the bramble and the bunnies, too?

Check it out.

LIFE IN THE COUNTRY – C. 1988

When I finished grad school in psych at Naropa University in Boulder, my wife, Maria, was pregnant with our first child, and as we were both originally from New York, we headed back East like migratory animals. For a variety of reasons that I shan't go into just yet, we ultimately landed in the storied, bucolic, and very tiny town of Woodstock, NY. Did we have a pretty clear idea as to why we were going there? Yes. Did we share the heart's-blood of it with our parents? No. Did we have a game plan in mind to make the whole endeavor stable and strong? Maybe. Kind of. Okay, no, not really. What I can say without equivocation, however, is that Maria and I were good kids, 25 years of age, and for the previous four years had cheerfully and independently moved through the universe together. First, San Francisco where we worked, had fun, and saved a little. Then Boulder where we did further studies. Now Woodstock to try our hand at living in the country and raising a family. Every step of the way, it is fair to say, our yen for adventure and awakening had led us onward.

Some of the older generation judged this harshly.

I recall Maria's grandfather (F.W.) sending her a scathing letter as per her residing in the "hippy" West, studying Montessori education (*what did Maria Montessori know about education anyway? she was a medical doctor!*) and marrying some dude (that'd be me). In response, Maria tucked the letter back in its original envelope, wrote a terse note to the effect of "Did you actually read this before sending it to me? This is unacceptable, Grandpa..." and sent it back to him. Curiously, that catapulted her to most respected status among his grandchildren: He thought she was brilliant!

The letter paid further dividends during the above-mentioned time of relocating to the greatest hippy town of them all, the true mothership, Woodstock, NY. Not a peep was heard from Grandpa then. But that does not mean all would be quiet on the Eastern front. I needed a job. And with my freshly minted Masters of Arts degree (Contemplative Psychotherapy) in tow, I cannot report that the job offers had my telephone ringing off the hook. I was not worried, though; and, somewhat fatefully, I did not look or seem worried. From a public relations point of view—correction, from a family relations point of view—I forgot that others might misinterpret my confidence as laziness, foolishness, or just plain taking my eye off the ball. Anyway, the precarious value of the MA was not news to me. Indeed, in case you aren't familiar with the field of psychotherapy and its hierarchy, an MA in Psych occupies the lower rungs on the ladder. You have modest professional choices, at least in the beginning of your clinical career. Think: Therapist gigs at community mental health centers. You also get skinny economic love in what (last I looked) is an industry that already pays modestly. Mediocre lawyers and junior financial analysts, by comparison, often make considerably larger sums. I don't mean to cry you a river, only to point to an American fact of life: *We live in a capital-biased culture.* In this instance, the profession that—at its best—focuses on human connection and provides antidotes to loneliness, cluelessness, trauma, and neurosis, gets a pretty low economic valuation in the marketplace. Might this values regime change over time? Perhaps. Might the capital mindset mature over time? Hope so. But for our purposes, let's put it in the "things as they are" bucket. In 21st-century America, the capital side of life remains robust and far-reaching, and it has its ineluctable requirements. Each Young Person will ultimately have to make his/her own sense of it; decide what to accept and reject; and live with the consequences. This gives further expression to what I refer to as the economics of selfhood.

THE LEGEND OF THE RENT ... (WAS REAL HARD CORE.)
Wait, what? The economics of selfhood? Come on. Let's take a much earthier tone: *Sounds like Wynn McFlynn needs a job.* Indeed, as stated a moment ago, that was true for me, winter of 1988. I had secured Maria and myself a new place to live in Woodstock; now I needed a job. I note that order because my

father-in-law, Svend, a man known for his gentility, bonhomie, and soft-spoken manner, went dark—in a devastatingly silent, Scandinavian way—upon my sharing with him the "good news" that I'd signed a lease for some sweet digs in Woodstock. At the time Svend and I were making our way up 7th Avenue. The NY Rangers hockey team had just lost a dull affair to the Vancouver Canucks, and now our destination was Grand Central Station and the train back to Rye. The night was bone-chillingly cold, par for New York in January. I did not realize that something was terribly wrong. Svend took a long time to respond to my declaration of good news. I had forgotten so much about the Old Home Ground where people had expectations on how things were done and why. Living in the West for seven years will do that to a person. Then Svend remedied that. In a low, tremulous voice, one that the Vikings must have used when feeling murderous, he said, "You know, in my day we got the job first, then signed a lease and moved there."

I don't consider myself overly sensitive but maybe I am. The words hit me like a sword. Smite is the word that comes to mind. *What an unbelievable screw-up was I.* The train ride back to Rye was a virtual blackout for me. For real. Once home, I took to my bed. For three days and three nights I was feverish like a character out of a Dostoevsky novel (and just as pathetic, I'm sure). It was bad enough that I was a bona fide knucklehead; but, much worse, I performed this extended inglorious act of feverish contrition in front of my in-laws with whom I was staying during this time of job search and new home search. Och! Neither you nor I needs a master's in psych to diagnose what was going on. I was freaking.

SOME REFLECTIONS, ALL MELLOWIZED
BY MY OWN PSYCHOTHERAPY

Now, thirty years after The Smite (okay, I did manage to bounce back), and now, as the father of a twenty-something daughter (with my own set of expectations for her would-be partner), I recognize the protective ferocity that a father naturally feels for his daughter. Still, it felt a bit heavy-handed. It wasn't like I'd ever been lazy. I'd always had a job—two, sometimes three at a time—through high school and college and even grad school, and that meant I'd always had a few bucks in my pocket. To find myself in the penalty box, smarting from said blow and serving what felt like a ten-minute major, was a bit bewildering. What had I missed? Was signing a lease before getting a job that big a deal? Or, was there more to the story?

Obviously.

Now the storyline primarily becomes one of geography and generational perspective.

This is to say: If you grew up in Rye, NY and for even a nanosecond thought about what's expected of you, only an immensely stubborn person would miss the unwritten graffiti written all over town and especially on the walls of Rye High School. I mean, the whole Rye High School building complex was modeled after Princeton University campus. Hello? Had I lost my glasses? I don't think so. Was I of questionable intelligence? I hope not. But indeed I was a fully committed goddam independent (aka GDI) and I wasn't buying the whole capital-first approach to adult life and in this regard living in the West suited me perfectly. The thing was, I wasn't living in the American West anymore, and getting hit by a sword on 7th Avenue enlightened me of that geographical fact. And this brings me back to comment on the generational perspective thing.

Like many of my parents' generation and ilk, Svend communicated a capital-first logic to things. Do whatever it takes to be a good earner, and provide for one's family. This was the first order of business in adulthood and family life. Getting the money/career thing on track accordingly got the lion's share of one's time, energy, and efforts. Everything else would have to wait its turn until that part of life was strong and stable. Assume, moreover, that this would take years to pull off, and include making significant personal sacrifices. This capital-first approach had its wisdom. It did not underestimate how fiercely competitive the capital side of life can be. And it had its benefits. It's economically potent to track like this. I say that with no condescension. For, gaining economic independence is no small shakes for any young person.

As for myself, no two ways about it: I was a goddam independent. I wasn't trying to be a GDI, I just couldn't help being myself, and, well, I was fine with that. At the same time this doesn't mean I was opposed to the capital side of life. I wasn't. I'd grown up surrounded by entrepreneurs and had always known that one day the family blessing/curse of entrepreneurship awaited me. But apropos the capital-first logic, I was clearly coming at things from a different angle. It went like this. First choose a path of aliveness and adventure; then figure out the rest. I did not know back then that one day I'd belong to what the demographic consultant and author Richard Florida later categorized as the Creative Class. I did not know then that many of my peer group were doing the exact same thing: Envisioning a life and moving to the city or the country to make that life happen, and then figuring out the rest!

In retrospect, I have no doubt that Svend was quite right to lower the boom when and as he did. The capital world does deserve one's proper attention. It's tough out there. But there was an opportunity lost, too. There was a much bigger conversation that could have gone down. Svend would have had to be super-skillful to pull it off, of course. The minefields of possible misunderstanding were everywhere, and I was never going to surrender the vision that Maria and I had for our life—a vision that was unique and genuine and heartfelt. But at the same time, there were wild blind spots and troves of missing data points. I had many things to learn concerning the world as it was. And in regards to the practical economic side of life, I definitely needed someone to wrestle me to the ground: *What's your game plan, Mark? Your vision is fine, or perhaps in need of refining. But the question remains: How are you going to make it so? For starters, do you have a budget?* This would have been the start of a different kind of financial education, one that begins with selfhood and adventure and romantic love, and goes from there. That different kind of financial education, one that is markedly more rounded, is the subject of this guidebook for the guides. To follow are anecdotes, snapshots, ideas, questions, and suggestions, as well as the occasional dollop of gossip to give us a feeling for what other good folks might be going through in their families. I hope some of it will resonate with you and your situation.

Listen, I will be honest with you,

I do not offer the old smooth prizes, but offer rough new prizes,

These are the days that must happen to you ...

— WALT WHITMAN

Chapter 3 # Open Road (money included)

It's fine that Walt Whitman breezed over financial realities in his rousing and lyrical invocation, *Song of the Open Road*. Great poets sing for all time. Like love itself, perhaps even like the follow-your-bliss ditty, their songs push us out into the world, to see what's there, to see what's inside us, and to try things on for size. But such poetic exhortation does not mean that now all in life spontaneously falls into place. *Au contraire*. Having a plan, charting one's course, recognizing the developmental tasks before us (or in this case, our kid)—all might be regarded as practical and, well, yes, a good idea. It makes no sense to talk about becoming our own person, or taking to the open road, if we ignore the character and influence and tasks associated with the journey in general and money in particular.

AGENDAS AHOY

My best understanding of the essential elements or tasks at play in the twenty-something decade brings me here, to think in terms of the *five agendas*, which are as follows:

- ➤ autonomy (both financial and psychological)
- ➤ adventure
- ➤ family
- ➤ passion/gift
- ➤ romantic love

I believe this list goes on the map of each and every young person. Of course, where a specific agenda gets placed, and why, depends primarily on the kid and what's important to him or her. We as parents/guides/bankers figure into the charting equation, as well. Our own financial goals may simply not accommodate the kind of underwriting that our kid seeks. Our own values may diverge such that we say, *Hey, that's your thing. It's important to you, but not to me. You figure it out.* Or, we simply don't understand a particular project, and decide to pass on it. Or, we still feel a bit frosty about how our support in the not-too-distant past was misused, and keep the purse shut for a while. And that's all a part of the rich mix as we huddle together to chart aspects and objectives of the journey. To be sure, there are many paths to success. At the same time, there's no skipping over things. Each agenda demands its time in the sun. Our kid will do well to gather the facts, and discuss, and deliberate. That's what this decade is about. It is both leisurely and full of room to try things, and yet it moves quickly and precious time can be lost.

Our success as guide depends in large part on two acts, ostensibly opposing yet complementary: That of good planning and that of nifty improvising. Planning I regard as a mode of thinking. Planning is a mode of conversing. It is ongoing. No one-shot deal suffices. To this planning "end" I think in terms of maps and map-making. I invite you to do the same. It will be within this structure of *visual-thought*, this cartography of self and the world, that you'll thread the planning discussions with your son, daughter, niece, nephew, godson, or grandchild. Naturally, you'll tailor things to fit with each kid's emerging sense of self. Tailor and revise. Equally, you'll improvise. You'll try things. Improvisation does not just belong to the denizens of jazz or stand-up comedy. It is that great creative act that all good parents rely on with astonishing frequency ... pretty much every step of the way!

· · · · · · ·

In a few short chapters, I'll provide you with something of a white paper on the five agendas or tasks of the open road, but first allow me to sketch a few brief notes on the cast of characters. Spencer, Jane Jr., and Quixotic Caitlin are front and center, and we'll check in on them as they meet with both the inspiration and challenges of the open road. Their stories are uniquely their own. In Part Two a few more people join the party. There, you'll see my college-age daughter, Taia, give me the proverbial run for the money, while my son, Mikyo, requires me to raise my game and get exceedingly clear on how I want to support his launch toward autonomy. In sum, the stories of these young people are intended to remind us how the journey and its delicious challenges fill up our young people and—to employ a bit of Whitman logic— how the young people in turn fill up the journey and its delicious challenges.

1.   **Spencer, age 22, musician, Boulder, CO:** College wasn't his thing. No big deal. Super smart kid. Warrior-type, in the good sense. Upright. Trustworthy. Without a moment's hesitation, I would've gone into business with Spencer. But he was no businessman. He played the kit like a demon. He tapped the high hat as sweet as sweet can be. Mid-teens onward Spencer moved with a couple of rock bands, one with real possibility, the other mostly a party. His relationship to money during this time—well, it was kind of like bad hygiene and forgetting to brush one's teeth. His parents were pretty nice about it. Still and all, the world was Spencer's oyster. Hugely talented drummer. Time for him to further his musical education and to see what the coolest cats in the universe were up to. Naturally, the money stuff side of his life would need a serious upgrade.

2.   **Jane Jr., age 27, paralegal, Boston, MA:** This young woman had her act together. Tick all five boxes? Financially independent: Check. Adventure: Had her fair share, check. Relations with family of origin: In a good way, check. Passion/gift: Ready to attend law school in the fall; a long time dream, all the more confirmed by her paralegal experience; check. Love: She and Beau were engaged to be married, check. Except love threw Jane Jr. a nasty curve. My daughter said it was nothing. *Get over it. Tell him: No!* My wife felt the wild complexity of it, and has yet to weigh in on the matter. Jane Jr.'s mom (Jane Sr.) was seriously angsting. Jane Jr. was feeling sick. As to the curveball in question: Jane Jr.'s fiancé (Beau) thought perhaps she could forego law school and they could start a family now and um, er, like, she could be a stay at home mom.

3.   **Quixotic Caitlin, age 29, second in command at local arts not-for-profit, though not for much longer, Boulder, CO:** Caitlin was a pip. Living in the finished basement of her parent's home did not remotely inhibit her penchant for hatching lavish, expansive plans, all of which fell under the title of Her Next Big Life Move. Fiercely independent? You bet. Well, maybe not. It's not that living at home as you are about to turn 30 is a crime, or even an intrinsically negative marker. But, by her own account, she did want more than this. Only she didn't care to be the one to make it so. She had other more exciting agendas to attend to. You know where I'm going with this?

4.   **Mark, age twentysomething, being a GDI in Woodstock, NY:** I had my wild blind spots, and a few cherished ideas that might rightly be labeled magical thinking. For long periods of time I flew low, really low. My instruments weren't working, or I wasn't paying attention to them, and my math was a tad confused. A "plan" for a family of four is a far cry from a plan for a family of two. Not that I had a plan. Before the day was done I'd scare the bejeezus out of myself. But I've leapt way ahead.

ACTION IS CHARACTER

Money and finances are embedded in the thousand decisions that each Young Person must make. I'd like to name a few. There are decisions about adventure and education and love and autonomy and pursuing one's passions and talents. These decisions (and the ensuing actions) come to define our Young Person's character and life's journey. How then can we artfully address these threads of money and finance? What are the lessons worth teaching on planning, implementing, saving, spending and the like? And, as importantly, how do we get them to stick, to become lifelong habits? Where is the middle way, between ignoring and over-amplifying the matters at hand? Where is the personal way that suits you and your son, daughter, godchild—of whom you are so fond?

My twenty-something daughter thinks the personal way has something to do with renewing the lease on her apartment (yes, I know, it's a what-goes-around-comes-around story!). My twenty-something son thinks it has something to do with busting the budget by dint of inhaling Thai takeout three nights a week. Jane Jr. finds herself wrestling with a feminism 1.0 conundrum: To delay, or perhaps ditch, the next leg up in her career for the sake of marriage and family, or no? Quixotic Caitlin thinks feminism in all its iterations is moderately lame and that the personal way is Her Magical Mystery Way. And, well, as we'll see on the next page, my godson Spencer thinks the personal way has something to do with New Orleans and meeting up with Kermit and Stanton and the cool cats down yonder. So let's head in that direction. We'll take in a few snapshots of Spencer, and then take stock of Jane Jr. and Quixotic Caitlin, before digging into how the heck we might help them to map their respective Open Road Journeys, money included.

Can you hear the brass band swingin' it?

That's our cue. Let's tootle on down.

  # Song of Spencer

In a trice I'll break out the family photo album from the high school years when my godson Spencer played drums and my son Mikyo played guitar in the basement, cranking the Marshall amps and shaking the bones of our saltbox home on a regular basis for a handful of years. Apologies for taking full advantage of the situation, but by cornering you with a few pages from the family photo album, I also intend to make the point that Spencer's present yen for a musical adventure is no impulse *du jour*. There was a long and winding road that logically and at times maddeningly led up to this moment of Spencer trying to figure out just how to make the big life move from Boulder to New Orleans. And, in case I haven't shouted it out lately: The boy could play.

Here again is my list of the five agendas or tasks of the open road, each with a note that applies to Spencer and his situation:

> **Autonomy:** Develop *métier* / put himself to the test / gain economic independence

- ➤ **Adventure**: Leave his comfort zone; explore the
  artist's life
- ➤ **Family**: Loves his parents; wants to leave home in the
  "right" way
- ➤ **Passion and gift**: The boy's got musical chops; but how
  good? time to find out
- ➤ **Romantic love**: Hello, Leah

In a few chapters thence, we'll take the time to describe in more thoughtful detail what each of these Open Road agendas means for Spencer, Jane Jr., et al. In so doing, I'll comment on how some agendas dovetail nicely with each other, while others blatantly compete for precious time, energy, and resources. Obviously, the economics of being a drummer, by comparison, makes my story about the economics of being a psychotherapist look pretty promising. But before I tumble down that rabbit hole, let's go back to beginnings, to Boulder, Colorado, not long after the turn of the millennium.

BAND IN THE BASEMENT (CIRCA 2003)

Before the surrender I had had my Saturday afternoon routine of zazen practice. Sounds exotic. It's not. Just good old sitting zen. Butt on cushion, legs crossed, candle lit, pine incense burning, and room otherwise quiet. As for my mind—Jeez, Louise. It could make such a racket. Think garbage truck in the alley at five in the morning. Where does the garbage go? Where does it come from? Is a mind a terrible thing to waste? I don't know. My meditation—well, let's just say I was no Bodhidharma. Still, I had very much liked that routine.

Then there was the band in the basement. It happened

suddenly. Practice had been at Spenny's house. He was the drummer, and damn proficient at that. Seems he actually liked to practice. Liked rock 'n' roll more than school or golf. Practiced all the time in his dad's woodworking shop out back and this drove their elderly neighbor (Peggy) to the brink of madness. Where she teetered. Until the full band gathered in the woodshop and practiced for what was one unrelentingly wet dark snowy spring season, and the band rocked it hard, and Peggy teetered no more. In fact, she fell. She fell into madness and did what no one does anymore: She called the cops.

Next thing I knew our house was a sort of weekend Rock 'n' Roll Humane Society. The band took up residence in the basement. Insouciant teenage girls (the self-appointed groupies) had their feet up on the living room furniture, and—between cell phone calls and text messages—had no qualms about making their every need known. Mercifully, Band Members and Homeowners alike were in no mood, and swiftly showed the groupies the door. But the sonic intensity did not let up. The Marshall amps and Ludwig Vistalite drum kit (yes, the John Bonham kit) pounded the bones of our home like the hammer of a great giant. That took some getting used to. Indeed, I thought I might change up my Saturday routine, maybe catch up on some reading, or head out and play a little golf. And on occasion, I did. But in the end I relented.

I did not see that coming—this surrender to just being around and listening to the band from my perch two floors above, while I put my feet up on my bed and got our bird dog Lucy to curl up next to me. Lucy was as sweet and earnest as a warm cinnamon bun could possibly be beneath the quilt. Regarding the music, in the beginning the jury was out. The band had mic issues and reverb issues, and the bass player, the first of many, was bad.

But Spencer and Mikyo worked their craft long and hard, and the band warmed to me, or I to them, and at some point it was difficult for me to understand how Old Peggy had gone bonkers. Our bird dog Lucy had an altogether different take on this, however. Since she wore her nervous system on the outside, she felt it all was much too much. But she was pretty sweet about it. In the main she lodged her complaints directly with Spenny, the drummer, during breaks. Fortunately, Lucy had the Dog Nature. Never one to hold a grudge long, never one to seek revenge or demand an apology, all she required was a little ear-scratching love and then she'd be lavishing Spenny with sniffs and licks and quivering hindquarter wags that were her equivalent of two thumbs up.

Lucy really wasn't too keen on this Song of the Open Road business, either. But I was. My father-DNA told me that now was the time for me to really pay attention. To tune in. In many ways the band in the basement made this easier, ensuring that many of the life events of these hormonally charged years would play out before me. I was glad of that. And the electric blues soundtrack to all this—well, you know the times have changed and changed for the better when, instead of someone getting harped on to turn down the music, you and your kid share musical taste and both of you are inclined to *turn it up*.

Spencer On the Verge (circa 2011)

Some years later, Spencer, 22, was ripe to explore the bayous of New Orleans and the life of the artist. He sought me out to discuss. It was obvious that his intent was sincere and this time he wanted to get it right. Multiple conversations ensued. Overtly thinking in terms of the five agendas of the Open Road (*autonomy, adventure, family, passion/gift, romantic love*), he and I surveyed the terrain of two basic questions: *What do you want in regards to a, b, or c agenda?* And: *How best to make that a reality?* In the case of Spencer, you might assume that because he was an avid musician, it had been clear-cut that he should pursue and develop his artistic gift. But it did not play like that. At the end of high school, Spencer enrolled at CU Boulder. His classes were interesting enough and his grades were good, but by all accounts he was a fish out of water. He wanted to play his music, and to a degree did, but the idea of studying music in an academic setting seemed sterile to him.

Wisely, and with the blessing of his parents, Spencer dematriculated from CU. His next move, however, was far from inspired. He entered what might lovingly be called The Hazy Period of Experimentation & Languishment. This included an 18-month residency in his dad's woodworking shed—residency as in sleeping there. Exactly when the thunderbolt of self-insight & life-direction struck him is hard to say, but even the least observant of people would agree that a prolonged stint with Stunningly Mediocre Band w/ Horrible Self-Absorbed Lead Singer *compounded by* waiting on hundreds upon hundreds of tables at the local Italian restaurant were contributing factors to his awakening. For Spencer, doing stuff he disliked was as "data relevant" as being aware of his own talent and passions.

What felt different about the New Orleans plan, at least to my mind, was that this time Spencer was headstrong in a *mature* way. That was real news. Heretofore, he'd made up his mind on X or Y plan, and that was that. No discussion. Little debriefing afterward. But not this time around. He systematically garnered the counsel and support of those around him—his parents, his brother, his serious girlfriend, and his kit drum teacher in NOLA. This spoke volumes to his desire, his awakening. Spencer wanted to learn from the musical masters. He wanted a shot at the big time. The time seemed right. *Let's figure it out.*

Chapter 5 Thoreau Plays the Backbeat

Overplayed is the motif of the starving artist. And yet, some artists starve much more elegantly and effectively than others. Arguably the causes for this are many, but right now I'm going to make the plug that there is one cause above all others; namely, *personal responsibility*. Or, to go colloquial: It's about choosing to get one's head in the game.

Spencer didn't get a free pass from the capital side of life, no matter how fun or noble or eccentric the cause. If he refused to deal, he'd likely end up back in his dad's woodworking shop. Here, I'm taking a page out of Henry David Thoreau's book. Whether the young Thoreau needed to learn similar lessons, I do wonder. It's true, we only know him later in life as a paragon of self-reliance and rugged individualism, as the scathing critic of what he perceived to be the vapid material excesses and technological distractions of his generation. Whatever the real backstory is, the legacy of Thoreau burns brightly. Autonomy was his middle name. He much preferred the life of the mind—what he dubbed the "real work"—but he also quite vigorously took economic responsibility for his life, and wrote fastidiously to that effect.

I wished for Spencer the same sort of tenacity and commitment.

But let's hit the pause button on his journey, and pop in on someone (Jane Jr.) who thus far appeared to be making short work of the capital side of things.

Chapter 6 # Song of Jane Jr.

Time now to quit the bayou, and linger not one second more in the Concord woods, but mosey on up the road to Boston and Beacon Hill, where we find Jane Jr., an astute young woman whose journey was uniquely her own. I say the latter bit knowing full well that her path and her life appeared—from the outside, looking in—mainstream and conventional: She worked as a paralegal, had law school ambitions; lived in perky digs on Beacon Hill, and planned to make her own way up the socioeconomic ladder; had a serious guy, and wanted to have children one day—might even consider being a stay-at-home mom; and so on. And that's all right. Sense of direction on the open road of life needs to correspond with inner truth and genuine curiosity. Irrelevant is whether the path taken looks socially conforming or not. Of course, our kid may have to skillfully adapt his/her act to meet the requirements of the world. In the case of Jane Jr. (aka Janie), the path taken indeed conformed in many ways to the world she grew up in, and it had also become—without contrivance, without mental gymnastics—genuinely her own.

As per the agendas of the Open Road, Jane Jr. (age 28) was

getting it done, and, I might add, in stellar fashion. Indeed, she was pretty handily ticking all the boxes:

- ➤ **Autonomy**: Was financially independent; had a healthy sense of self
- ➤ **Adventure**: Even if a local girl, living in the city still fit the bill
- ➤ **Romance**: Dug her guy; though trouble was speeding right at her, as we'll see
- ➤ **Gift/Passion**: Work in progress; had her eye on the target, but ...
- ➤ **Family**: Family of origin was proud and supportive; was building a life with Beau ...

Now, prior to all this, there were the bumps in the road. For two years Janie had had to survive working for a wretched excuse of a human being—so dubbed The Trunchbull—who took as much of the joy as she possibly could from Janie's workday. This, we know, happens. Workplaces can be dens of neurosis and psychosis. Anyway, Janie fought through it and got to the right side of it, and then for the last couple of years had been cruising along.

However, Life threw her another curve. This one was considerably more perplexing than her experience working under The Trunchbull. It's also saying a lot because being a lifelong Boston Red Sox fan, Janie knew a thing or two about curve balls. It was only recently that the Sox had broken the 80-year-plus Curse of the Bambino. Even so, as a player in her own twenty-something life, she didn't see it coming. Part of the issue was that the pitcher was Love. The other part of the issue is that Life is full of the unexpected, and the unexpected comes, well, when and where you least expect.

It was a damn nasty curveball, if you ask me. Here is her story.

THE PROPOSAL

After an all-accomplishing time at one of those gem New England Small Colleges that cost her parents a small fortune, Janie now lived and flourished in Boston, and did so with a mix of conventional sensibility *and* her own truly individual spiritedness. More recently, after a four-year stint as a paralegal at one of the top law firms in town, Janie's intuitions were confirmed: She loved the field of law, found herself endlessly fascinated by it, and was gearing up to attend one of the top schools, which she had recently gotten into.

Then Beau proposed. This delighted and surprised her. She said yes. And the big news rang out. Everyone—both families, close friends—reveled in the love. What's not to love about Love? As to the once dreamy discussions between her and Beau of their shared future, that too seemed cause for gaiety, song, and dance. No one saw, as often happens, the thunderheads gathering in the distance. No one heard the lightning crackling overhead, until Beau laid out his scenario, sincere and practical, for having and doing family. You might recall from your own life, it concerns the highly complex, highly emotional discussion of roles and responsibilities. But Beau could have written a dissertation on his vision, that's how well thought out and serious he was. Janie did not see this coming. Not this quickly. Then there was a profusion of chaos.

THE OTHER PROPOSAL

Evidently, Jane Jr. aka Janie wasn't the only one doing well for herself. Beau (30) had recently finished his PhD in molecular cellular biology at MIT, and Wall Street money managers and headhunters were texting him night and day with lucrative job offers.

No such thing as a sure thing, but Beau's *hunterly* prospects were looking pretty good at this moment in time; and, well, he and Janie weren't getting any younger; so perhaps they didn't want to wait too long before starting a family? Or, so Beau sweetly and logically opined. In a matter of seconds, however, the discussion burst out into the open. Would Janie consider being a stay-at-home mom?

She would. Sure ... one day. She was in no rush, though. But, sure, she could roll with that. She wanted to more or less be a stay-at-home mom ... one day!

Beau pressed his point. He had some serious job offers on the table. The pay was insanely good, and would cover their life together, and that included a growing family. Perhaps they should do a strong division of labor arrangement, with Beau assuming the role of prime hunter and Janie as prime parent/mom ... not one day ... but sooner?

But that'd mean she'd have to ditch the 3-year law school plan.

Yes, he understood that he was asking her to consider delaying or altogether ditching her law school plan.

Gulp.

. . . .

Jane Jr. did not immediately reject what Beau put forward. She loved her guy but now she felt like she'd overdosed on crazy pills. She needed time to think it through and get clear on what she wanted, but both time and thinking seemed to make matters worse. Jane Jr. felt afraid that the wrong answer might one day cost her everything with Beau. She knew this was irrational and ridiculous. But was it? To her mom, she wondered aloud if she'd stumbled upon some heretofore unknown pocket of low self-esteem in the caverns of her psyche. It all had her spinning. The winds were kicking up in all directions. She did not want to sell herself short. But why did she feel so responsible for making sure their new family life would work? Was Beau asking her to do that, or was he merely putting his detailed vision of "family" into the mix? Or, was this his anxiety-driven need to put things in order so that he could relax and dive deep into whatever gig he finally settled on? If so, would he secretly resent her for carrying on with her endeavors? Evidently there was a slew of calls from daughter to mother that began: "Crazy pills alert! Mom, we've got to talk. Do you have a minute?"

Chapter 7 Song of Quixotic Caitlin

In regards to bringing order out of the chaos created by an abundance of love, honesty, economic prowess, and options for how to do love and family—no doubt, many folks would assert these are the "good" life problems. And they are. And they're still hard. The choices are often quite perplexing. But not everyone sees it that way, like my dear Quixotic Caitlin, 29. She unabashedly pines for these problems. She'd love for Love to solve the autonomy leg of the journey. *The open road is not all it's cracked up to be!* And while we're making a list (which she freely assumes means "wish list"), Caitlin would also like her next big Adventure (i.e., voyage to New Zealand, think *Lord of the Rings*) to magnetize Mr. Awesome Guy and solve her longing for Love. *Why the heck not? As I always say, Ask and ye shall receive ... though, Take and ye shall receive is an excellent Plan B!* Considering these facts alone, you can see it's not a great stretch on my part to assert that Caitlin's perspective of the world differs rather dramatically from the one attributed to Jane Jr.

Is Caitlin's magical love manifesto a put-on? I think not. *Just make it manifest* is something of a mantra for her. Lifelong, it hasn't hurt that she's terribly clever, stubborn, and unreasonably good-looking. The world has often bent to her whims and wishes. Even so, how's all this working out for her? Where is her Romeo? What do her mind and heart whisper to her in the quiet, alone moments of life? And assuming love really is bendable to someone's will, does it also then provide the hall pass to roam, to skip out on the twenty-something tasks of separation and individuation? Does receiving an *incomplete* in self-reliance matter? What about doing a no-show on one's talents/passions—does it matter? As it stands now, Caitlin seems enchanted by her own modernist version of the fairy tale.

I'm skeptical.

. . . .

Below I offer snippets of conversation taken from a recent get together with Caitlin. The tone of familiarity between us reflects the fact that we've known each other a dozen-plus years, thanks to her Aunt Zoe. During the past seven years Caitlin and I have met a handful of times specifically to discuss her life and planning and money.

ONE RING TO RULE THEM ALL

"I just tendered my resignation at the Arts Center. Gave them two months' notice," Caitlin said.

This was news. I was aware she'd done a superb job coordinating programs there for the past four years. After college, it had been her first serious job.

"The politics became insufferable," Caitlin went on. "I'm so

burnt. I just have to return to New Zealand. My spirit feels so …
thin at the moment. But not everyone thinks so. Zoe—my aunt,
as you know—is my best friend in the whole wide world, but she
disapproved of my plan. Said I must be smoking a big fat one …
which for the record is not my vice of choice. All I know is I want
off the grid. Not sure for how long. Maybe a year. Last time there
I had such a good time."

Last time there she'd fallen in love. Ian was his name. It had
seemed serious for a while. Don't know the details of how it ended.

"Well, you're her financial guy. She said if I can get this past
you, then she'd stop the harangues!"

Did she now?

"I mean, Zoe is right. I'm 29 and living at home and it's pretty
embarrassing and all. And, by the way, besides the stress of dealing with the new Executive Director who was an odd ball, how
was I ever going to make my own life living on 40k a year—in
Boulder of all places? I could cover rent and taxes and food, and
that's about it. What kind of life is that? I told my boss I needed
44k a year. She laughed and said: 'You're not serious, are you?'
I told her I've never been more serious in my life. She turned and
walked away, as if I'd said nothing, and I was left standing there
… like, really! I fumed for one long weekend and then tendered
my resignation."

I wished she'd kept her job long enough to find a new one.
But that was not on the docket. Nor would it be.

"I've got 40k in mutual funds that my grandmother in L.A.
gifted me. I figure I can take 25k of it and go to Auckland and
study pottery for the year with this amazing guild of potters
there."

Yes, duly noted, that Quixotic Caitlin yen for adventure!

But I was also reminded how the last time Caitlin and I had

formally met to discuss her life she was all aflame with Ian (an Aucklander) and thinking that he might move Stateside or she might go to New Zealand, or they might agree on something in the middle—like live in Ireland! Not long after that, I met Ian when he came to visit. Seemed like a good chap. However, upon learning that the romance flamed out, I could not help but entertain the cynical thought that once Ian had gotten over here and saw that Caitlin was doing okay but was still living at home, and that she came from some means but definitely wasn't some absurdly rich American girl (i.e., the proverbial writing on the wall hinted that he might find himself on the economic hook to pay for their shared life journey if they married); perhaps in the face of that, Ian turned and sprinted the heck out of the relationship.

Just one man's guess.

"Love's important to me. I'd like a life partner. I'd like to have a family one day soon. And I worry. I'm 29. It depresses me some. I feel the clock ticking. And living in my parents' house doesn't help matters. I feel a little ashamed I'm still home."

I wasn't necessarily buying that last bit. Living at home in middle-/upper-middle class America was no badge of shame—not automatically, anyway.

I asked after the capital side of her life. What kind of prospects did she envision for herself when she returned from this adventure and re-entered the workforce? Would the economics of it be more compelling then, or would it ensure a return to her "apartment" in her folks' home?

"I knew you'd ask that!"

I kept at it. Were there tools or trainings that she wanted to gather in this next period of her life? Was there merit in getting right back in the job market while her stock was still good? I too heard the clock ticking, though in a different way.[1]

"You're a real downer," she said brightly. "My Aunt Zoe likes you, why? But seriously: What if this time around I find real love?!?! I just feel that it's out there right now, coming toward me."

For twenty or so seconds we sat in silence with these words bouncing around the chatter-buzz café space. Finally, I looked at Caitlin and said:

"You did hear what you just said, right?"

She smiled.

---

1 I buy into the thesis of the UC Berkeley trained psychologist, Meg Jay, that this indeed is a ripe time of life for change; and that it feels more or less true that it's very hard to change the big stuff—career, love, other—after age 35.

Chapter 8 # Mapping the Open Road

In good time I will challenge Quixotic Caitlin in her attempts to magically *bypass* the demands of the journey. In maneuvering as such, she is not alone. *Bypassing* goes in many directions, flashing red-alert when there is a particular agenda of the open road that a young person would prefer to do without. Quixotic Caitlin actually had several agendas that she wanted to fly over and, donning white gloves, wave down to them in an Audrey Hepburn kind of way. I myself was not without my own *trip* back in the day. I was hedging. There was a stubborn streak in me that wanted to give the capital side of life the precise minimum to do the job, and nothing more. Problem was, my math was faulty. My calculations about the capital world were missing variables, and perhaps most fatally were a tad egocentric. Had it just been Maria and me and life in the country, the money we made would have been more than enough, but we had the kids and we had zealous ideas on their education. Only later, at the ripe old age of 30, would I realize that I needed to get my financial life substantially more robust and disciplined, and that meant going into capital-overdrive to make up for lost time. Not fun!

In stark contrast to the imprecise hedging efforts of me or the galaxy-hopping efforts of Caitlin, is Freddie First Born. I don't think we'll hang with him much in the course of this essay, but he represents the young person who immediately takes to "the straight and narrow path." Arguably, his is anything-but-the-open-road journey. These matters of individuation interest him little, at least right now. Singular is his focus. At the age of 24, indeed, he's taking the train into the city, and subscribing to the capital-first program. Sure, he fits the old stereotype, what with his wearing the sharp flannel biz suit and carrying the old leather briefcase, but, in spirit, he could just as easily trade places with the dude wearing jeans, black t-shirt, skater sneakers, mangy backpack, and working eighty hours a week at QZQ Emerging Company in the SF Mission, or Brooklyn, etc. They share a mindset. "Growing up," to them, is primarily a financial, material matter. Get the career in overdrive, make some serious bucks, and one day get the identity perks and social status of financial success. May take ten years, may take longer. That's okay too, or so Freddie feels now.

Whether Freddie First Born is bypassing the Open Road journey altogether is outside the scope of things now, though I will say there are a lot of fine young people who feel they must strongly overweight their time and energy to "success" in the domain of career and doing well for themselves financially. Regarding this set of kids, I don't have some blanket judgment. I've seen kids grow up in families, good families, that were often financially out of control, and the kids felt stressed out about it and vowed, *I'm never going through that again.* Very human, and understandable. I've also seen kids genuinely jazzed by the hubbub of the marketplace; who wanted to play the capital game and be one of its big winners. The game held great allure for them. I've seen kids as well who keyed on entrepreneurship, who had a vision for innovative products and services and the delivery of them. Despite my initial resistance, I would become one of them. And, as many of us entrepreneur nut-heads know, the entrepreneurial road can be long and at times all-consuming. So I wish to dash any notion that my ethic is high-flying or privileged. Anything but! Succeeding on the capital side of life, and I say this leaving a lot of berth for countless variations of what financial self-reliance and robustness might mean, remains a major undertaking for any person.

To be clear, I regard the process of becoming one's own person in this world (aka individuation) as top of the list. All is subordinate to this emergence of self and spirit, except I certainly hope it does not stop there. I hope that is *the end of the beginning,* to borrow Churchill's phrase. I hope the young people take their full sense of self and strong confidence of having a place in this world, and extend that out to benefit their partner, their family members, their friends, and others in this world. I include the planet in that extending out.

But enough of my exhortations: I'd like now to formally develop the framework for you and for us to be superior guides. As such, it'd be ideal for us and our kid to speak the same language, and use the same tools of *visual-thought* to think about and, when the time is right, chart a given course. Balances must be struck. There should be room to focus on specific plans, and develop them in depth, yet there should also be reminders of what not to shunt, what not to stubbornly or innocently or charmingly bypass. The idea here isn't to tell our kid where to go, but rather to help with the measuring and planning and strategizing. Agendas on the open road of life tend to get arranged by the passions of the present. Nothing wrong with that, so long as we, in our role as guide (and part-time banker) also insert well-placed comments on the long view, to wit, that some agendas have an "arc quality" to them. Indeed, such agendas are developed step by step over time ... or, fatefully, they're not.

. . . .

To come now is an exposition of the Open Road. Mapping is the method. In subsequent chapters we'll bring this mapping framework with us as we revisit and think more deeply into the particular stories of Spencer, Janie, Caitlin, and my younger self. Sailing in and through too will be breezier visits with Alexandra, Josh, Wynn, Nate, Mikyo, Taia, and perhaps even again with Freddie First Born. But without further ado, let's carry on with this formal side of our Open Road exploration, starting with *autonomy* (psychological, then economic) and followed by *adventure, family, passion/gift,* and *romantic love.*

Here is a fuller description of each agenda:

Autonomy Part I (psychological):
Independence takes vision, imagination, moxie, and money. In its simplest terms, personal autonomy combines the outer aspect of economy with the inner aspect of psyche. We need sufficient quantities of both. To be our own person in this world, we have to know what we're about. In popular culture this is referred to as selfhood. Carl Jung, the 20th-century Swiss psychiatrist, used the term individuation, which he described as a lifelong path toward psychic wholeness. I've always thought of this as akin to the notion, "to be a rounded person." Either way, there's no final, static "that's me for all eternity" place of arrival. If only! Life incessantly

bumps into us; we into it. All kinds of ideas are tried on for size. Some fit, some don't. And with that new data we revise and update our sense of who we are and what the world is about.

This dynamic nexus of "self"—of becoming our own person—is made up of a grand plurality: Self-identity, emotional intelligence, judgment, personal happiness, social intelligence, values, genuineness/self-recognition, and character. Nothing here springs forth by its own accord. To achieve a kind of inner fluency in matters of the self—well, that takes care, attention, exertion and friends. Being our own person on this inner level is a great (and vastly underrated) accomplishment.

AUTONOMY PART II (economic):
Making a literal, physical place for oneself in this world is also a great accomplishment. I refer to the side of autonomy that concerns itself with money and economy—aka the capital side of life. For many young people the "accomplishment" of economic independence takes time. It develops as a matter of degree, and we as principals of the Bank of Mom & Dad (or Aunt or Friend) may underwrite a portion of what's going on. This is the case for Alexandra. Right out of college she received, after a couple rounds of gritty negotiation, $400/month extra support from her family. This helped her make ends meet since the pay at her cool job was modest while the local rents were expensive. Of course, such help (even the kind rooted in love) is not "free." Alexandra found herself accountable to her parents and the budget they all crafted. A deal's a deal. Still, I think it fair to say that Alexandra was and is *mostly* independent now.

For a splash of contrast, there's Wynn McFlynn and his story of alternation. He was killing it in Brooklyn—or so he reported—acting and filmmaking and waiting tables. But now, for the second time, he's burrowed back in the basement of his parents' suburban home. What happened? Did he catch some bad luck out there with George, Lennie, and the rabbits? Or did he party like it's 1999, and now he's broke? Or did he miscalculate the cost of video editing? Or a mix of all of the above? For the parents of Wynn, these vicissitudes are painful and perplexing, and definitely wearing thin. In the realm of economic autonomy, there's no denying Wynn is not getting it done. He's in the seriously dependent camp.

To come are more stories and snapshots from the open road. The cardinal point here is that economic autonomy often takes time, and, as we've seen with Jane Jr., can include nettlesome twists and turns for even the most accomplishing of the bunch. I should also note that apropos this matter of our kid getting financial support from the Bank of Mom & Dad, I offer no all-encompassing answer. Giving/getting support can be a blessing or a curse. It can be highly appropriate or highly inappropriate. It can empower or distract. The god or the devil is in the details. The terms of the contract should be specific to who our kid is and where his/her head is at. Not least, the terms should work for us, aka the bank.

I would be remiss to not quickly mention (again) that in the course of this inquiry (in Part Two) we'll be sure to dig into the practical arts of personal finance: *saving, spending, planning, implementing,* and *investing.* We'll also delve into what I regard as the subtle arts of personal finance—i.e., making sense of *cognitive styles, behavioral patterns, critical judgment,* and *typological factors.* Now, though, let's carry on with the formal introduction to the remaining four agendas of the open road.

ADVENTURE:

Do *Europe On $5 a Day*? All right, I'm referencing my woefully out-of-date 1980 edition of the student travel bible, but you get my drift. What's the plan? What's the adventure? This is the time. This is the decade. Josh is mulling over a grand plan. Ship the Ducati over to Le Havre and buzz all over the continent. Excellent plan. Figure it out, fund it, do it. Once he checks in to medical school, the window of opportunity for adventure closes for a while. Then there is Taia. It's the summer before she finishes college, and she's thinking it's time to sit *dathun*, the vaunted month-long buddhist meditation retreat. Talk about rugged adventure. Conrad Anker has got nothing on anyone who can climb the nasty, formidable "inner" Mt. Meru that is known as dathun. Dear Taia, go for it. You're 22. When else are you so easily going to be able to get off the grid for a month?

This is the ideal decade to try things, to see the world, before all manner of commitments come to define our kid's life. By the way, the verb "to try" has at its root the Old French verb *trier* ("to sift") and this seems wonderfully apropos. My buddy, Red, who was an intrepid entrepreneur and philosopher-cat, said: *Try anything and everything in the decade of your twenties. The decade of your thirties, however, is all about focusing on one or two things.* This feels basically true. Failures and mistakes and wrong turns are less critically important in one's twenties. Naturally, they still sting, but most of these experiences carry with them the sweet possibility of redemption. Of waking up. In other words, what is critically important isn't good grades, so to speak, but how good a student of life our kid is. Will she lean in and examine the data of experience? Will she learn from both victories and defeats? The biologist Lewis Thomas wrote that we humans are actually wired to make mistakes. A curious statement, but his argument is nonetheless compelling. Making mistakes is the quickest and most trustworthy way to gain info and learn all manner of life lessons, and the evolution of our species evidently depends on it.[2]

Adventure is where we test our self, and test our (oft semi-conscious) hypotheses about our friends and the world. Under its sun we often sweat bullets of fear and joy simultaneously. These tests cannot be skipped. No way to know who we are without them. But they can be arduous. The edges can be very sharp, and cut deeply. We might not feel ready. More to the point, our kid might not feel ready. But adventure also cuts away parts of the self that we later learn we can do without. Layers of habitual self-doubt get cut away. Layers of habitual self-deception get cut away. Distinctions are made. The path of least resistance, for instance, proves not to necessarily be the right path. That cutting away, that shedding of skins, seems quite necessary. It makes room for new possibilities. It makes room for self-reliance. Then drinking from the cup of life tastes that much more refreshing. We recognize the value of what we have. We recognize the value of this present moment called our life.

FAMILY:

First, there's family of origin. In the lives of our kids, indeed, we are just that. We are their family of origin, which is to say, our young people must "separate" from us! Earlier I used the Jungian phrase individuation—to become an individual. Now I borrow kindred phrasing from the field of family therapy; that is, separation/individuation. I like the term. It feels complete, inclusive of the positive and the negative, like rose and thorns. The point is, there is a sorting out process for the young people regarding values and ideas and so on. In order for them to be their own *agents*,

---

2 Thomas, Lewis. *Lives of a Cell: Notes of a Biology Watcher.* New York: Penguin Random House, Inc., 1978.

the young people must truly exert to arrive at their own distinct sense of things. Some of this may coincide with our views and values, and some may not.

Additionally, not only are the young people sorting out what's what for themselves, we ourselves are simultaneously sorting out *our* relationship to *their* journey. This is done out of love as well as self-interest. We have agendas of our own, after all, and we have to be smart with our finite resources—be they emotional, energetic, or economic. Independence may be on the rise for the kids, but often times we have them on belay. If they fall, they land in our lap or in their old bedroom. On the other hand, we shan't exempt ourselves from what's going on. If our marriage is falling apart, or we are experiencing postpartum depression in regards to the kids being gone, *and* we aren't dealing with these realities, then we should not be surprised if the young people feel the weight of that, too.

In addition to family of origin, there is the new family that our young people, of free will and amorous activities, create. This expression of family can take the form of marriage (or civil union) between two people, or the more expansive arrangement of marriage + children; or, configure as one adult with child/children. By all means, one should add in dear friends to "family" if that fits. At any rate, these configurations fall under the header of family, and here we find *social contracts* galore. Whether anyone has read the gross or fine print of said contracts is another story. Usually the terms are clarified later, amid the din of battle, when there has been a grand collision of expectations as per roles and responsibilities. Even so, no one seems especially deterred by this. The evolving arrangement we call family seems to be bumping along, and clearly it works for a merry band of twentysomethings. I know it did for me. Just loved family life from the get-go.

Found great delight and inspiration and peace of mind. Other folks feel no interest whatsoever in making a new family, and that's all right, too. All I'm angling for now is to underscore the obvious: This is a very social and relational domain, characterized by not only responsibility, but the never-ending social math also known as the give-and-take.

PASSION, GIFT:
Passion/Gift points to that electric node of talent & calling. Seemingly, the muse chooses our kid as much as our kid chooses the muse. This was true for Spencer, though his was hardly an instantaneous realization. It took Spencer some time (and languishment) to work up to the fact that he loathed college and was wasting his time in the (then) current rock band. Once he realized that, it took another swatch of time (and languishment) to figure out his next move—i.e., time to go to New Orleans and learn from the masters. This standing on the "threshold" is classic. Knowing what one wants, I mean really getting down to the bones of what one wants, even in a domain where one brims with talent, is hard. Adventure is fun and all, and failures can be laughed off amid great storytelling ... to a point! Spencer hit that point. It was as if he'd needed to wear out his particular rock 'n' roll fantasy, to get down to what the life of the artist might really mean. *Play great music and live just above the poverty line? Cool, or not cool?* The unknowns were ubiquitous. Going to New Orleans wasn't just about living the dream. The seriousness with which he planned his Boulder to New Orleans move was auspicious.

Of course, our understanding of passion/gift extends well beyond the cultural arts. To have and to do *meaningful work* belongs under the banner of the artful life. Now, there could be the temptation to read into my words some statement of moral high ground, but I'm not a fan of dividing the world into the ostensible do-gooders and everyone else. I'm a fan of authenticity. So I'm applying the most subjective possible interpretation of the phrase; that is, doing work that is deeply meaningful *to our kid*. And I think we can trust this subjectivity, regard it as a sane platform for living a full and interesting and compassionate life, as opposed to taking the view that "what's meaningful to me" fosters selfishness or feeds narcissism. Sure, that's possible. It's possible that choosing the artist's path is a real personal trip, or trying to save the planet is a cop-out from facing the earthy realities (i.e., paying the rent and food bills) of life in the decade of one's twenties. But then that is another matter altogether, and surely you and I will unflinchingly challenge that if we suspect as much.

ROMANTIC LOVE:

Love is mercurial. It's also a change agent like no other. This can be a good thing, or a destructive thing, or—as is the case much of the time—to be determined. In my own family, whenever our son or daughter dated someone, I made it a point to be observant, yet to reserve judgment. It was their social life, after all. It was their experience to make sense of. But in the course of my letting go— an act, I might add, that I needed to do repeatedly—I was not silent. I offered each child my sharpest, best-cutting diamond. It came in the form of a question. *Do the two of you (you and your boyfriend/girlfriend) bring out the best in each other?* The occasional lover's quarrel or brooding that I witnessed, the implied sexual intimacy based on their emotional connection, the delight they took in each other's bad jokes—none of that concerned me. For the most part it seemed healthy, but, really, it wasn't for me to judge; it was for them to judge. *Do you and your boyfriend/girlfriend bring out the best in each other?* That, to my mind, was the standard. It was my sincere wish that they—my young people—adopt that as their standard.

Love is frightfully random. There are those stretches of time in life when love is nowhere to be seen. Of all the agendas on the open road of twenty-something life, finding romantic love consistently operates beyond the reach of willfulness and strategy. Our kid can put himself out there, take repeated social risks and the like, and still come up empty handed. The only thing he can control is whether he puts himself in circulation, although even that—if it goes on for too long—can feel like a bad joke. On the other hand, love's math is basic. It takes but one person, one partner, to suddenly make it come alive.

Arguably more problematic than being love-struck or being depressed about absence of love, is getting caught in the web of "love that is half dead." This is the relationship purgatory where young people waste precious time and energy. The open road of life gets smaller, more narrow. They stay together, but, in and through the relationship, they're not learning and growing. This mode lends itself to bad decision-making. The classic mistake, the all too prevalent mistake, is to live together (aka cohabiting) for the wrong reasons, such as: 1) it's convenient 2) it seems financially easier 3) no other options look more appealing 4) the world seems like a crazy place—i.e., bolt the door, I quit the world!, and 5) maybe this is the best I/we can do. Evidently, this major couples "decision" is commonly made without much of a discussion. In fact, early research seems to substantiate the claim that cohabiting in this informal, semi-dull way is a terrible idea.[3] Over time these relationships tend to lack resilience, and fall apart. This runs counter to the short term, hopeful appearance of things. For instance, cohabiting does seem to "solve" issues of

---

3 We've relied on Dr. Meg Jay's vetting of said research in her April 14, 2012 NY Times piece, "The Downside of Cohabiting Before Marriage."

economic autonomy. Sharing the bills and having two incomes in theory should help. Something similar can be said for matters of selfhood and self-identity. Being in a relationship, belonging to a relationship, does immediately give one an identity and a recognizable spot in the social scene. However, long term, any unfinished matters of selfhood often find a way to sabotage the relationship. In sum, the "union" of two half people is inherently unstable. For love, as wild and enlivening as it is, requires the stability, strength, and clarity that only two rounded/whole people can bring to it.

. . . .

Now let's take this cartographer's open-design approach and see how it might apply to each of the main characters in our Open Road cast. Spencer, you may recall, had a New Orleans plan in mind. But unlike his prior excursions in which the plan was really no-plan, this time he systematically gathered the provisions and intel he'd need for the journey before going forth. Motivation for this upgrade in approach came from all corners. Almost as important as making it in NOLA, was the motivation to not end up living back in his dad's woodworking shop. Then there was Jane Jr.; how quickly and strangely her fortunes turned! Last we checked, she had the emotionally-charged task of clarifying how her individual journey would intertwine with married life. Perhaps this struggle was normal these days? Or, perhaps it existed of her own making? Moving on, we also grabbed a spot of tea with Quixotic Caitlin, a willful young woman who was waving her wand and playing with the magical fabric of the universe. If anyone could unravel things, if anyone could defy gravity, it'd be Caitlin. But my money remains on gravity. And, while I'm in the betting spirit, there were the bets placed by my younger self. Looking back, I appreciate my stubborn ideals and what I was pushing up against. However, that sort of ambition, the kind that respected the capital side of life but at the same time refused to be owned by it, meant that I had to be canny as all get out; canny as Thoreau; and, well, I wasn't yet canny as all get out; and I'd just have to find that out for myself. Without further ado then, let's take those earlier narrative sketches and fill out the picture with the color, texture, and elemental definition that the five agendas of the open road offer up.

Chapter 9 # Map of Spencer

Below I summarize a summer's worth of conversations, four in all, that Spencer and I had on the front porch of my house, where we scarfed down my wife's insanely good bacon cheeseburgers and talked freely, posing questions, identifying what data was missing, and trying on for size various communications strategies for him to his parents. The conversations weren't simply about getting from Point A (Boulder) to Point B (New Orleans.) Neither were they just about the economics of the adventure, although as you'll momentarily see I wasn't terribly subtle either. We focused intensely on his goals, yet made it a point to pan back and consider the broader context. Heeding the call of the muse topped his list. That harmonized with his yen for adventure. His parents loved him and in general were behind him. Something similar could be said for his girlfriend. But, as expected, the economics looked daunting. He would have some very real financial issues to think into—a process I'd help with, but my help would incorporate healthy doses of skepticism. As I've mentioned, the Follow Your Bliss motto might be fine for gathering one's courage and starting things off, but it's a poor guide for dealing with the brass-tacks realities of the journey. So I did my level best, in my rather uncomplicated role as godfather to Spencer, to both encourage him and rain on his parade. Having a well-developed cranky side himself, Spencer was more than up to my challenges:

- ➤ What about the economic life of the drummer? Let's talk real numbers. Who gets paid what? What does Stanton Moore make? What does Terrence Higgins make? Per gig? Per teaching class? Per royalty?
- ➤ Now, even if you turn out to be the greatest drummer of all time, you surely know musicians are a dime a dozen and are perhaps the most deeply discounted commodity on the face of this American earth: What about that? Again, let's discuss who gets paid what on the pecking order. Let's also discuss how long things take to move up the ladder.
- ➤ Are you cool with being semi-poor for the next several years, if not longer? What are your thoughts about having the proverbial day job?
- ➤ Are you okay with the possible outcome that your musical talents aren't up to snuff, and you could find yourself returning home and re-inhabiting your dad's woodshop again?
- ➤ Even more complex: Because your parents will likely assist you financially, what do you owe them in turn? Do we have details? What are the terms?
- ➤ What do you say about your past financial transgressions— i.e., you've worked a lot, made a lot, but have only a little cash in your pocket? What are the lessons to be learned? What's changed in you, or not?
- ➤ What are the dos and don'ts when enlisting some level of financial backing from your folks? Have you made promises you likely won't keep? Did you get them to commit to a fixed

amount as a potential loan, or did you leave that nebulous? Did you show them your plan, as well as disclose what you have and what you owe others?

➤ And as if that weren't dizzying enough, there's the not so small matter of romantic love. Is your serious girlfriend coming? Should she come? What does she expect of you? What do you expect of her? And that includes money, of course!

. . . .

Here now are my post-conversation notes, formatted in terms of the five agendas:

Autonomy: At this point in his life Spencer was not economically independent. Nor was he wholly dependent. He did possess a real work ethic, and made decent money waiting tables. Where that money went, however, was a topic of intense discussion. When he had had a goal that required money, Spencer had saved accordingly. This explained his acquisition of first-rate musical equipment, his travels to NOLA for Jazz Fest, numerous weeks touring with Stunningly Mediocre Band, as well as procuring at auction the lime green Ford pickup truck from the US Forest Service. But save funds for one day, rainy or sunny, in the future? No, he had not done that.

Everyone (namely, his parents) had hoped that his current "residency" in his dad's woodworking studio, going on 18 months now, would remedy the situation. Seemed like the ideal set up (i.e., paying no rent, living in semi-uncomfortable quarters) for saving. How explicit all parties were about this is unclear. My guess is that his parents were plenty clear and Spencer had other things on his mind. Anyway, that's water under the bridge. When the Moment of Inspiration arrived, the savings of this blues-rock drummer were nil.

Spencer knew this looked pretty bad.

That's probably why he at long last consulted me.

The New Orleans plan was consuming him, he just had to pull it off, and that meant he'd have to approach his parents for some financial assistance to make his move.

In my role as planner friend I was blunt. First, he'd have to fix things with his folks. Throw himself on the mercy of the court. He'd been a knucklehead, so cop to that. No excuses. If he could do that, I'd help him with the second piece, which wasn't small either. Sure, he needed a game plan, but as importantly, he and I needed to work together to develop a set of strategies to reform his habits around spending, saving, budgeting as well as planning. Did he agree?

Spencer agreed with little protest.

On the matter of psychological autonomy, I'll keep my comments brief. At the top of the list—my list, anyway—was that this was a real character moment for Spencer. He'd been acting like a wild young man, and now was the time for him own up to his history of non-seriousness around money. Next on the list came the call for some down to earth self-insight. Spencer acknowledged he'd never had a clue where his cash went, and that his cluelessness had to stop. This willingness to ding his own ego was a sign of maturity. No doubt, an assist went to his parents and where they drew the line on "help." Sleeping in the woodworking shop wasn't terrible. It had heat, and a decent enough mattress. But it wasn't all homey either. Spencer said he'd like to avoid doing more time in the woodworking shop if he could help it. Taking responsibility to learn how to do money was a good step in a new direction. I think the motivations that Spencer's parents left in place for him were subtly brilliant.

The domain of autonomy was one that Spencer would do well to bring real attention and effort to, especially the economic side of it, or it could plague him in all the other agendas of his life.

Adventure: Heeding the call of the muse, giving himself fully to developing his passion/gifts around music, harmonized easily with his inclination to adventure. Spencer liked taking risks. Always had. And, if you added in his musical interests, New Orleans was the logical next spot on the geographical map. It had the abundance of musical talent, old and young, who collaborated and composed and gigged together. Johnny Vidacovich. Terence Higgins. Stanton Moore, et al. Some of these masters also taught the finer points of their craft. You might say it was a passing on of the oral tradition/torch kind of thing. In order to get into this revered "institution," no one needed to take the SATs or write an essay for a college application. Rather, one needed an introduction, a personal point of connection. Spencer had that. That was the in. Then, if they liked you, if you had heart and talent and a work ethic, they'd teach you didactically or by putting you on the spot—moving you from the drum tech job to sitting in the drummer's chair in the middle of a gig. It was easy to imagine that Spencer would be in his element. Indeed, this time he'd be a fish in water.

Everyone has an agenda or two that doesn't come easy, or that requires extra work and attention. Adventure brings with it some sharp edges, as well as excitement and fun, and it certainly intimidates a cross section of young people. Spencer wasn't one of them. In need of money? Yes. Afraid to leap into the unknown of adventure? No. Taking to the open road for the sake of his musical path represented a natural progression. A natural leap. In choosing New Orleans as his destination, he headed straight toward the bright lights, where he'd put himself to the test to see how he'd measure up.

Family: I don't have a ton to add here. Spencer came from a very supportive family. They loved him and wanted him to pursue his dreams. He loved them and recognized their support and knew he needed to take better care of the relationship; to wit, by taking better care of himself. That life phase of impetuosity and languishment was over. Now risks and opportunity would be measured as best as possible. Spencer owed that to his parents. He owed that to himself. I believe he indeed was going about things in the right way.

In sum, Spencer saw the wear and tear he had at times put on his family of origin. Now he resolved to raise his game.

Passion/Gift: This was the nexus of all his open road activity. It was the prime mover. Spencer was pretty naturally aligned to these energies. Nothing more to add here.

Romantic Love: This was another part of Spencer's life that bubbled along with relative fluidity. No pining for love. No wondering whether he'll one day connect with her. He'd already connected with her, and she with him. I'm sure the relationship had its moments, they all do, but Spencer and Leah seemed pretty tight. Seemed pretty supportive of each other. Seemed to really enjoy each other. But, as for the details, no, I'd like to punt on that.

. . . .

The thing that stands out about Spencer's story is that so much seems to wheel off of his Passion/Gift agenda. And, while this kind of organizing principle can provide a feeling of clarity, the key is to not let the other agendas fall by the wayside. I think these conversations with Spencer bore some fruit, for he is now looking at the artist's life (his) through a wider-angle lens.

 # Thoreau Plays the Backbeat (Reprise)

I'd like to restate an earlier theme. Some artists, yogis, bodhisatt-vas, and goddamn independents, starve much more elegantly and effectively than others. Arguably the causes for this are many, but I think bottom-line it has to do with the level of responsibility a person takes, combined with the cultivation of a kind of capital *shrewdness*. As previously mentioned, Henry David Thoreau had this combination in spades. In the opening chapter of his seminal work, *Life in the Woods* aka *Walden*,[4] Thoreau bores us to tears with his lists of cost of goods purchased, sale of goods at market-place, cost to live his life, etc. He even calculates, and boasts to us, that he must put in 42 days of manual labor to be free to do as he pleases with the other 323 days of the year. I can't help but think of this as a wonderful display of transcendental common sense.

Much, though, is not known. Did Thoreau have longer-term plans—i.e., beyond his detailed subsistence plans? Don't know. And what about the economic underpinnings of his life? For two years he encamped on the land by Walden Pond, care of the lar-gesse of its owner, who also happened to be his sage older friend,

---

4 Thoreau, Henry David. *Walden; or, Life in the Woods*. Boston: Ticknor and Fields, 1854.

Ralph Waldo Emerson. But did Thoreau have substantial assets in the bank, or under his mattress? Was he the beneficiary of a trust? Don't know, but obviously these matters impact how wild an adventure any one of us might take. Still, there's no denying Thoreau was, economically speaking, a resourceful and conscientious devil. And as such, I make a declaration in his name. That is, I declare that artists and intellectuals and yogis and bodhisattvas—i.e., those with the least materialistic ambition—should be the most canny in the domains of personal finance and career/work.

Our kids want to be free? Great, then earn that freedom. Then defend that freedom. Be masters of the economic realm. Be sharp, be creative, be attuned. They don't need to be the richest or the most paranoid, but they do need to be self-reliant and know where in a capital society the leverage points are. This, then, is my express wish for my godson Spencer: To sharpen his mind and strengthen his commitment and gather the skills; which is to say, to take a page out of Thoreau's book and become outrageously economically savvy.

> *"I went to the woods because I wished to live deliberately, to front only the essential facts of life, and see if I could not learn what it had to teach, and not, when I came to die, discover that I had not lived."*

> —HENRY DAVID THOREAU, *Walden* (1854)

Chapter 11 # Map of Jane Jr.

You may recall the quandary Jane Jr. (aka Janie) suddenly found herself in. Her fiancé, Beau, was chock full of ideas for how and when to do the family thing. On one level, it was all pretty guileless and sweet, except his vision of family worked at cross-purposes to Janie's next big life move: Law school. Such give-and-take is an ordinary part of family life. Even so, there's no denying the stakes are incredibly high. Decisions made today have a way of reverberating far into the future. Looking at matters through the lens of history, moreover, it is clear that the person who ends up playing the supporting role in marriage occupies a vulnerable spot in the family system. And the terms of modern love haven't fundamentally changed this particular relationship clause. Sure, the revisions with regards to "equality" in marriage are much improved, but none of that changes the fact that Jane Jr. was being asked to forego her individual dreams and her future earnings-power. I myself didn't like it. Nor did Janie's mom. But we'll stand down for now.

Let's map out the journey of the Open Road, though this time account for the rugged topography of modern love. Somehow, Two Individuals endeavor to become One Team while at the same time remaining Two Individuals. Got it? Good. Also, I should disclaim a bit here. Some of my commentary presumes a modicum of accuracy from Jane's mom (aka Jane Sr.) and her rendering of things. I myself have never found Jane Sr. to be particularly dramatic, but this is her daughter, after all, and I thought you should know the source. Still, I'm not that worried about Jane Sr.'s potential distortion field, because I think the story is less about the personal details and more about this wonderful and highly complex shift in our kids' lives—i.e., getting married or committing deeply to a relationship. Perhaps, too, it reveals the angst that many of us parents feel at such a juncture; angst about the limitations of our ability to help our kids, and angst about how the postmodern world still (at least to me) wrestles with the demons of the past. Anyway, let's leap into things with some questions:

Does marriage usher in the end of the Open Road journey?
I think not, though all concerned parties should expect to see some heavy revisions on their individual map. Still, the timing of said heavy revising is hardly uniform. In the case of Jane Jr. & Beau, they dove into the deep end forthwith. A tad unusual. Seems like more often than not the young-and-in-love get down the road of life a ways before they hash out these terms. But there's no right answer. The timing is personal to the couple.

Will these heavy revisions be equitable?
Fair question. Not sure. Also, hard to measure. The effects of some decisions play out over long arcs of time. Only time reveals if the revisions were "fair enough" for everyone.

Will each then do the same tasks?

Probably not. Division of labor (e.g., you do the dishes, I vacuum) is quite the effective mode of co-journeying. Of course, it exists on a continuum, and slides along as a matter of degree in relationships. But here is the funny thing. From what I've read (studies cited in my second book, *Lion Hearted Love*), the more extreme divisions of labor (i.e., one person makes the big bucks, the other plays supporting role in home life and the family system) appear to occur more in relationships that stay together than in those that do the less extreme divisions! Now, which comes first? Does the stable relationship lead to the extreme division of labor? Or does the division of labor encourage the stable relationship? I really don't know. Nor am I particularly espousing any one configuration at this point in time. I think a voodoo priestess will bring much more value to this wild calculus of figuring out who can and should do what in the constantly brimming over and kaleidoscopic domain called family life. But I have wandered off. As per Jane Jr. & Beau, all I can say is: We found them in the deep end of a deep inquiry.

. . . .

Here are some further thoughts on Janie & Beau, the matter of revising the map, and the kind of negotiations that might accompany this shift from "solo" journey to "ensemble."

To the agenda of **Adventure**, the young people should count on geographic twists and turns regarding where to live as well as travel. Even after thoughtful negotiation, one or both will periodically get pushed out of their comfort zone. On the other hand, for some couples, this agenda flows easily and intuitively.

It's the heart center of their relationship. It enlivens them both, and yields the joy of camaraderie.

In regards to Janie & Beau, this wasn't an issue. Move to New York or stay in Beantown, they easily agreed on geography.

To **Family**, there is a very real shift. The "new" family created becomes like the sun, and the family of origin, the moon. Which is to say, putting major energy into the vision for their life together—for Janie & Beau—was now the primary family agenda. Establishing this new center, psychologically speaking, was and is a big deal; and should be regarded as a further expression of separation and differentiation from their parents.

Simultaneously there was the matter of what Janie & Beau wanted their family to be. The chorus of questions descended: How did they wish to grow their family, and why? What might this mean for each person's roles and responsibilities? Were there other personal agendas that would, as a result, be impacted or emphasized? More on this matter in the next chapter (Shouts & Murmurs), where a few friends discourse on gender.

To the agenda of **Autonomy**, there's the mind-bending shift from silo to ensemble approach to one's life. The risks inherent in this new "entity of two," along with its opportunities, are certainly worth noting. There will be sacrifices. Perhaps, financial sacrifices. Perhaps, career sacrifices. But surely, above all, there will be sacrifices of the self. This is the dance of ego amid relationship. This is the interplay of individual agendas amid the family ecosystem. This is the give-and-take of marriage, which ideally leads to its own set of opportunities. For, when a marriage is done well, there is the very real potential that $2 + 2 = 5$. This is true economically speaking. This is true in terms of sharing the peaks and valleys, as wells as the joys and comforts, of the journey. Not a bad potential payoff in my view.

Jane Jr. & Beau were focused on the right issues. The intensity of the discussion, and its division of labor negotiations, naturally tossed them into the deep end.

To **Passion/Gift**, there may be very real and reasonable pressures for one person to suspend, pare back, or forego his/her individual pursuits. Front and center are the couple's goals, and, within that, how to most effectively accomplish them. The latter could entail a sharp division of labor, as earlier broached. "You work the long hours and make the big bucks; I'll make a few bucks, and work the long hours to make family and home life perk along." Much as this looks like a throwback to my parents' and grandparents' era, it is radically different insofar as it is consciously chosen by partners with equal power in the relationship. As noted earlier, the allure of this approach is economic stability, if not prowess. Dividing-and-conquering actually works, and tends to bring the biggest economic benefit to the family. (And, as noted, it seems to appear in marriages that remain together.) Still, this mode of co-journeying is a huge deal. There are big risks to individual autonomy and adventure and passion/gift, but also big potential payoffs for the partnership. (I wrote extensively about this topic in *Lion Hearted Love*.)

T'was the heart of Jane Jr.'s quandary.

Did Beau get off scot-free?

No. The thing is, he had the economics on his side. He could make beaucoup bucks right now. It wasn't unreasonable of him to challenge the timetable for family. Nor did it preclude Jane Jr.'s agency. But that challenge certainly triggered memories of gender injustice and imbalances from a not too distant past.

I would be remiss not to mention how the agenda of family (and marriage) may well be an expression of passion/gift for some young people. Maria and I certainly felt that way. Early on, we felt the inner truth that evolving our relationship—supporting and encouraging each other, as well as shining a light on our less than winning aspects—was indeed inseparable from our spiritual paths.

To the agenda of **Romantic Love**, I don't think there's whole lot more to add at this time, except to underscore how romantic love is the great catalyst for personal learning, growing, and change. Conversely, it can also prove terribly destructive. The relationship could be rooted in evil, or neglect, or lack of skill, or one party's intractability. Highly complex are the negotiations about roles and responsibilities in the new partnership. I am reminded of a rather famous saying attributed to Confucius: *To know the seeds is to divine the outcome.* Therefore, negotiate well, Dear Young-People-In-Love!

Janie & Beau possessed the greatest riches in the universe—love, and genuine affection. They laughed at each other's jokes. They smelled right to each other. To borrow a phrase, they had the right stuff ... in matters of love and life and friendship. Now it was being put to the test, as life ineluctably will do.

Chapter 12 # Shouts & Murmurs

I don't know. People talk. We talk. On the home front I got some lively input from two of my favorite readers.

My twenty-something daughter, Taia, refused to buy into the big deal around Jane Jr. and the start-a-family decision. "Just tell him, No! He can wait till she's good and ready. Like in three years when she's done with law school."

My wife, Maria, agreed, though mostly voiced concern over the kind of schedule that Beau would likely need to keep, to succeed in a new high-powered job. "I don't have the answers, but I do know if Janie goes to law school and Beau launches his post-doctoral career at the same time, they're both going to be working crazy long hours ... and that's rough on any relationship. Things tend to fall apart. Who is going to do the laundry, pick up the dry cleaning, buy a few groceries, or file the taxes on time?"

To the rhetorical question, Taia replied, "Beau can do the laundry, pick up the dry cleaning, and so on. Not only that—he can chill out on the have-kids-now bossiness, and dial it back in his career. No one is making him go to New York and be a rock star and work stupid long hours. He's a big boy making big choices. Janie should go to law school. It's her passion. Sounds like she'd be a great lawyer. If Beau loves her like he says he does, then he needs to make some room for her. End of story."

On occasion in family life I know when to shut my mouth. This was one of them. I did not begin to posit the other side of the argument, the vulnerable side, that has women still feeling overwhelmingly more responsible for the success or failure of the (heterosexual) marital relationship than the man (drawing here on the work of Harvard psychologist, Carol Gilligan, in her groundbreaking work, *In a Different Voice*). Gender politics, acculturation, Stockholm syndrome, other—I'll leave it to The Erudite to explain the causes and conditions of this lingering phenomenon. However, I will state the obvious: 1) Human emotions are powerful, and 2) Emotional truths often occur whether we like it or not. As for how to challenge the causes and conditions, I'm going to stick to the material, to the economics of the situation. This is where we'll also find Jane Sr., with a stiff cocktail in hand.

One Negroni, One Martini with Jane Sr.

Janie's mom landed in the same camp as Taia, though for a set of reasons that spoke to the history of ugly divorce in our parents' generation: "Janie completely economically depending on Beau scares the bejeezus out of me. Understandably, she wants my input, but I don't know how to say what I want to say to her without her feeling undermined by me. I'm afraid for her. I'm haunted by the picture of Janie having two kids and one day the marriage tanks. Beau is a fine young man, no doubt about it. But marriages tank. Nice people become jackasses. What happens then? Fifteen years down the line, with a marriage crashed and a couple of kids in tow—no, then it'd be too late. She asks me: Should I ditch law school? I know my answer. No time like the present for Janie to go to law school. That's what I say."

I knew my answer, too.

I'd never wish to see my very willful and sparkly daughter, Taia, in an economically dependent position either. Whether this was a wisdom view or a neurotic view on my part, I couldn't say. But it was emotionally honest. I love my daughter. I'd never want to see her stay in a cruddy marriage for economic reasons. In moments I've skirted around the topic. One of these days I'll speak openly to her about it. And, having had numerous imaginary conversations with her, I'll be ready. My message will go like this:

*By all means choose whatever lifestyle you want IF and WHEN that family-with-kids day comes your way. But before then, which means sooner, please develop your talents. Become your own person. Learn to carry your own economic weight, and then some. Gather whatever professional chops and training are important to you. You are talented. Do not squander this time to develop your gifts. Even the most socially illiterate person can read what lies between these loving, yet cynical lines. Yes, it's true, my dear daughter, that by taking my advice, and going to law school or whatever, you'll have some good insurance in case things play badly in your marriage. You will have some real professional education and skills and chops to fall back on IF **things don't work out** ...*

Who wants to deliver that message while love holds great promise? Worse, how do you say to your kid who has found love and quite possibly a viable life partner that she will do well to buy some "insurance" for the future, um, well, just in case?

Made both brilliant and lucid by my negroni cocktail, I shared the short version of this soliloquy with Jane Sr., who seemed both lucid and brilliant herself.

"Cynical or not, that's precisely what I want to address. But I'm afraid I'll spoil what for her should be a happy time. On the other hand, she is asking me what I think! Ooof!"

While Jane Sr. *ooofed*, I thought of Taia's prior declaration: *Beau could dial it back in his career. He's a big boy making big decisions.* She did have a point. He was quite the ambitious chap. But now I kept my counsel to Jane Sr. as simple as I could: "Do tell Janie what you think. But don't get trapped in seeing this as a singular issue. It's not. You'll get shut down if all you express is your fear about her perhaps one day being left high and dry by Beau. There are hosts of other uncertainties about the future, many of which are basic, basic, basic. Agreed? Take Beau's future. That high-powered career path in New York may prove a terrible mismatch. He thought he was cut out of for it, but once there, it may not be what he wants at all. Or, he may love it but—yes, even for Beau—he may not be the right stuff. He may perform poorly. The unexpected has happened before to other talented people. It can happen to Beau. Or maybe it's not black and white at all. Beau moves around a little bit on the job front, and ends up at a job and a firm that he loves, but the pay is just all right. No problem. Why? Because Jane Jr. has her income stream care of her law practice, and the two of them are pretty glad about that. I like the idea of options for them, I really do, particularly since we know that the cost of a good life isn't going to get cheaper."

I don't think Jane Sr. heard a word I said. Only the olive was left in her martini glass, as she semi-whispered, presumably to herself: "There's no issue I'd rather tackle less. Where is Feminism 3.0 when you really need it?"

Allons! through struggles and wars!
The goal that was named cannot be countermanded.

Have the past struggles succeeded?
What has succeeded? yourself? your nation? Nature?
Now understand me well—it is provided in the essence of things
that from any fruition of success, no matter what, shall
come forth something to make a greater struggle necessary.

— Walt Whitman

Chapter 13 # Madness, Failure, Failure, and Madness

One recent fine day, while I was grinding to get in a few brokerage trades for my investment clients before the closing bell, my mobile phone buzzed and flashed with an incoming call. Although I knew I'd have to ignore it, curiosity got the better of me and I checked to see who it was. Nate is a young man, around 26 years of age. I've been friends with him since the time he left home, which was about ten years ago. By "friends" I mean that he and I have a raft of mutual friends via the buddhist community with whom we've barbecued, drunk beer, and played poker. This crowd also loves to argue and watch baseball at the same time, which go surprisingly well together. Amid these rowdy gatherings Nate and I have had something of an ongoing Open Road type conversation, most often covering the terrain of work and potential business opportunities and the associated need for capital. All in all, I've had the impression that Nate has been resourceful as hell, taken good care of himself despite difficult early years, and been quite sincere in endeavoring to make something substantial out of his life. And yet, as I saw the phone ring and saw it was from Nate, I felt something. Call it ambivalence. Call it a tinge of exhaustion. I wasn't in a hurry to call him back. Why did I feel that way? It wasn't like he was my kid, or nephew, or godson. What was my aversion about? This, it would seem, was one of those relationships with a young person that I judged to be less than productive. More on this later.

I'm well aware that for much of this essay we've been on the train, rolling down the tracks, chugging all over the country, mapping everyone's Open Road journey. I'm also aware that my friends regard me as a lovable but annoying optimist, and, assuming this is true, I'm likely prone to not give the darkness and madness and obstacles and failures their proper due. So let's change it up. At the next station we'll get off and find some shade and have a Processing Moment for Us Guides. Specifically, I want to parse the dark and funky side. I also want to examine an array of limitations that can occur in the course of our big-hearted guide-work. You know, maybe we can't help our kid, or Nate, or Quixotic Caitlin through XYZ situation. If true, then is that the guide's fault—i.e., our fault? Or perhaps our kid is being insincere. Let me up the ante: What if in the first X number of years of our kid's life, we did a bang up good job as parents; and yet, here we are, unable to advance the ball or help our kid in regards to a specific, significant matter concerning the Open Road journey? What if Whitman is right, that in the essence of any fruition lies the seeds of a greater struggle? More, what if we can't provide meaningful guidance to our kid toward navigating some aspect of that greater struggle?

Being a guide isn't easy. There will be dark moments. There will be moments of pure bewilderment. Here are five thoughts to help dispel the fog of the open road, or at least provide a bit of solace. Humor is also allowed.

The Kid We Worry About (KWWA)

In the next chapter, where I'll pick up on the plight of Quixotic Caitlin, you will learn that in her family of origin she was indeed the kid her parents worried about. Being a smart cookie herself, Caitlin sensed this and thus seldom missed the opportunity to give them reason to worry. Yes, I know I'm being a bit snarky and simplistic here, so I'll get to the point. The temptation with the Kid We Worry About is—for us—to not hold the line in our dealings with them. Because we worry about them, because they seemingly or actually provide us with reasons to worry, we lower the bar; and, quite naturally it follows that, when they don't make it over that bar, we relent and revise downward in untold subtle ways. My counsel: Don't do that. If the KWWA doesn't perform, then don't give the goodies. Yes, it's that simple.

But it's not. The KWWA usually finds some very nerve wracking places and moments to struggle. What's more, he/she might even be a sweetie, totally open to our advice, but that changes nothing. The harder we try, the more creative we become—that also changes nothing. What to do? My rec: Be very thoughtful and precise and formal in whatever agreement we make with our kid—and stick to our end of it. Yes, that might mean Kristof doesn't receive matching funds for the post-college trip to Europe, in light of the fact that during the prior summer he failed to earn any money to match. Disappointing? Yes. But this, my dear friend and fellow guide, is a wonderfully accurate communication. This is a good thing.

In the next chapter on Quixotic Caitlin, I'll discuss the notion of economic tension. It's not the same dynamic equation for every kid; that'd make no sense because kids are so different from one another; but the basic idea is that we're not afraid to let our kids experience the economic truth of their life and their actions. If we shield them too much from that, then we should not be surprised by their low motivation and lame performance. Of course, there will be exceptions. There will be kids like Freddie First Born who need no parents holding them accountable, who indeed have been pining to wear the flannel biz suit and hop on the 7:12 train to work in the city starting the day after college graduation; but, kids like Freddie FB are the exception, not the rule. For the vast majority, it is through the experience of a certain amount of economic tension that our kids feel motivated to learn; to take notice; and that includes the Kid We Worry About. It almost goes without saying that in regards to the KWWA we'll predictably worry that he will be overwhelmed by the economic tension (i.e., anxiety) that he feels. My counsel: Don't give into that fear. Don't take the view that economic anxiety is crushing him and that's why he flails on the open road of life. That's probably not true. Rather than asserting this as the quantum answer to dealing with the KWWA, I'm suggesting this (our worry about his anxiety) as the weak link in our dealings that we will do well to fix as soon as possible.

THE KID WE WANT TO THROTTLE

Yes, we also love the KWWT. There's no denying that in moments we might want to send them away to reform school (!) or have them attend Envelope Pushers Anonymous meetings, but in and through it all our love for them is real. I know this first hand. In Part Two I'll discuss how I was no match for my 22-year-old daughter who, despite my firm and sage counsel, was on a sparkle-pony spending mission ... until she ran out of savings. She hit ground zero and then she had a little motivation to get real and it's fair to say we had some things to talk about.

The thing about the Kids We Want to Throttle is that their asset is their liability. Such bounty of willfulness will do them well in life, and yet, unharnessed, it can take them to some strange places. And that brings us to the throttle part. Not only are these kids known for plowing forward with their dang agenda, but they have this infuriating way of not hearing us. Whether they can't or won't hear it from us is always an interesting sidebar. But in terms of the guide playbook, what then must we do? Well, first, as noted, we do have to hold the line. This was true before with the kids we worry about, and it's true again. Naturally, it's true in all situations. An agreement is an agreement. No equivocating or renegotiating after the fact! Beyond that, I'm going to change up the guide playbook here and now. That is: Don't fight the willfulness. Sometimes our kid isn't going to hear it from us, and it doesn't matter why. What then? One idea: We draw a different and somewhat paradoxical line. We say: *Hey, I get it. For whatever reason, you don't want to discuss adventure, jobs, talents/gifts, love, and so on with me. That's okay. I'll let it go on one condition. Get a thought-partner. Find someone you like and respect, and who is at least five years older than you, and air out your ideas with that person. And, to be clear, the nice thing about having a thought-partner is: You owe him or her nothing. You don't have to do what they say. However, you'll still need to seriously think about what they say, so as to avoid being that person who likes to gripe but not really change some aspect of her life ... because then such good helpful people run the other way. Anyway, maybe I can't be a friend or counselor to you in matters of love or adventure or whatever. That's okay. But think about someone who can. It's actually a mark of maturity. It's what the smartest people do ... they air things out, they gather ideas and information, and then think about things before they make the next big decision and do it.*

PRIDE

I like Nate, and I know he's smart as a whip, and I appreciate the grit and decency he displayed in how he left home and made it on his own. I haven't yet called Nate back, but I will. In regards to why the hesitation on my part to call him back, it took me a while to put my finger on it: Nate has a slight excess of pride. He wants to talk about life and business, and likes to share his thoughts as well as solicit my own thinking on matters; but things are static. He tends to seek confirmation on his view of the world and what he already knows, whereas I'm interested in seeing him embark on the process of discovering the world that he doesn't know much about. This doubtless is an immaturity thing *and* an ego thing on his part. Nate rightly feels proud of his independence, and what he's accomplished and learned thus far. But he's ambivalent about going further. The vivid truth is this: To become a great student of the open road, to develop that muscle, he'll need to put his pride away. At this stage, learning begins in earnest the moment he realizes how much he *doesn't* know. What will lead to the moment of realization—I can't really say. I think it will come for Nate. I really do. But I won't have much to give him until that time comes, because in many ways my best ideas concern becoming a great student of the game. Answers mean little. But the questions, the mode of inquiry—on such matters I can definitely be a good friend to him. That is, if he'll let me.

BRAIN FARTS GALORE

Of late, I've been thinking about a couple of thorny situations involving the children of friends; and, after a considerable period of feeling stumped by the things I'd heard, I arrived at a modest yet durable insight: Kids who are 18 to 22 are wildly, insanely, and quantumly different from kids who are, say, 25 to 28 years old. Yes, it's the maturity thing. Yes, it's the shedding of one final thick layer of egocentrism. Yes, it lines up with what neuroscience tells us.[5] Our kid's brain doesn't complete the build-out on the neural power station until age 25 or so. Call me simple, or neurologically challenged, but this explains a lot. In the case of my kids and a host of other kids who definitely are "good kids"—likable, thoughtful, conscientious, and whatnot—I've been amazed by how they can perform world-class knuckleheaded maneuvers, seemingly out of the blue. You know, if I recorded a day-in-the-life series of moments, they'd look like this: Good, good, smart, cool, b-o-n-e-h-e-a-d-e-d, good, pretty good, and so on.

Periodically, there's an article in the media with ideas about how to make your kid financially literate from the cradle. Perhaps there's a small slice of truth to some of these ideas, but mostly it's ridiculous. In many ways our kids aren't developmentally ready to meet the big and intense challenges of life—i.e., the ones that they'll encounter on the open road—until their early- to mid-twenties. This isn't to let them off the hook. Nor does this mean we all drink beer and play skittles till then, though like baseball and arguing, that too sounds like a fun combo activity. Rather, we are the paragon of equanimity, which is to say: We address the 5% knuckle-headedness of our kid, and we also address the 95% light and goodness and openness of our kid. Brain farts will happen. In our house each kid got a "get out of jail free card." We did not tell them that in advance, but Maria and I had a feeling they might get used. We made it clear that each kid got a grand total of one of them. After that, they were welcome to land in their room and live by our rules if they really wanted to pretend that their brain

---

5 Siegel, Daniel J, MD. Brainstorm: *The Power and Purpose of the Teenage Brain.* New York: TarcherPerigee, 2014.

farts were something other than brain farts. I don't feel nostalgia for these moments ... though I'm super glad I was there for them.

Don't Regress in the Face of Madness

In your role as parent, guide, banker, you will assuredly experience swatches of madness and you will be tempted to regress to the level of your kid. Don't do it! I am reminded of one of the more profound lessons I learned about being a psychotherapist: Don't do the work for the client! Pretty basic idea, but when not yet a seasoned therapist, it's very easy to do. Why? Because the budding therapist is inclined to believe that "successful" treatment means that the problem gets fixed; and so she attempts to fix the problem because she wants to be a good therapist; but the problem belongs to the client, and the client—strangely enough—may or may not want to fix the problem. Really, the whole matter is up to the client; and any success in treatment hinges on the client deciding what he wants to do about it!

To restate: Don't do the work for your kid.

To which I will add: How do you know that you're the one doing the work? Because you'll be the one who is stressed out and pissed off about it while your kid probably won't be (except when you're raising your voice).

All of this is easier said than done, I know. It's hard to wait out someone whom we love. I care about Nate, and he's not my kid, and I'm slowly getting clear about how I want to engage there. Will I be a useful guide or thought-partner to him? I don't know. But I do know that I won't be going along with his desire for confirmation. Been there, done that. Which is fine. But I don't feel the need to do it again.

The earth, that is sufficient,

I do not want the constellations any nearer,

I know they are very well where they are,

I know they suffice for those who belong to them.

(Still here I carry my old delicious burdens,

I carry them, men and women, I carry them with me
    wherever I go,

I swear it is impossible for me to get rid of them,

I am fill'd with them, and I will fill them in return.)

— WALT WHITMAN

Chapter 14 # Delicious Burdens

It happens to us all. Sometimes, instead of being the impeccable guide, we get in the way. Sometimes, for reasons rooted in primal love, we interfere with (aka unwittingly help) the young people as they struggle with their burdens—burdens that belong to them, burdens that no one yet regards as delicious. But then we get it together. We catch ourselves, or our partner catches us, and we self-correct. We let go. We disown the struggle that rightfully belongs to our young person. Here, I'm officially broaching the topic of *economic tension*. Over time, and in varying degrees, we are the main managers of our kid's experience of economic tension. *I'll pay for college; you study and deliver good grades. You want a Vespa; you get a job and buy the Vespa; or not. You want to live at home after college, then here are the rules: Weekend nights home by 1a.m., contribute a few bucks to food, do dishes three nights a week, save _______ per month for the next life move, and so on.* If you prefer to substitute the words anxiety, stress, or burden for tension, that's fine. The point is, money is stressful. Economic matters are stressful. They require exertion. But that's only half of it. Learning to stabilize, to equalize in our being, some measure of economic tension is a good thing. It's a part of the human experience. It's a part of what it is to be an individual. Looking ahead, it is inevitable that one day we won't be managers of this tension at all. Life will go direct, and definitely happen to our kids. Money will then become for them what it has already become for us—a tad rude, though also full of interesting moments, like the guest that never leaves. The truth of this we don't need to ram down our kid's throat. On the other hand, much artfulness is required of us.

I suspect such artfulness was missing from Quixotic Caitlin's family picture. For, it seems fair to ask: As longstanding underwriters of Caitlin's life, might her parents have been supporting her in ways that unwittingly inclined her to extended bouts of strawberry-fields-forever type reverie, not to mention episodes of rather expensive flights of fancy? I don't mean to be harsh. The matter of help and financial support in a close-in relationship is highly nuanced. Even so, I think we will do well to develop a keen awareness of how our actions impact our particular kid. In my family one twenty-something kid took a little financial support and it went a long way toward strengthening his position of independence, while the other required a detailed negotiation about what the funds were for, followed by a real meeting of the minds on the overall plan. Neglect either of those steps, and we might find ourselves covering something else, such as the tragic gap in Child #2's wardrobe. Note: The Poor Child only had Steve Madden boots in mahogany, charcoal, and burgundy. Going without teal for so long, I imagine, had been a real character builder. Okay, enough of my dripping sarcasm, cathartic though it is!

The reason I bring the energetics of *economic tension* into relief is this: It's always operating, whether in the foreground or the background. How we in our role as parents and bankers shoulder some or all of a particular economic burden, how we transfer some or all of that to our kid—is very much at the heart of how and what we teach him or her. We all know well how pressure applied at the right time and in the right way (*i.e., rewards, support, or closing the purse or stepping back*) can suddenly turn a kid's creative, problem-solving mind toward the matter at hand, and often times with impressive results. We all also know of kids thrown into the deep end, who then sink to the bottom until fished out. Lesson learned from such trauma: Sinking sucks.

In sum, we as parents apply economic pressure through the relationship, and do so in whatever measure feels appropriate given who our kid is, where his or her head is at, what the specific issue is on the front burner, and what time of life he or she is in. But, nothing is guaranteed. Trial and error rule the day. And necessarily all of this is a dress rehearsal for the big time—for the world out there. Life takes money. Individuation takes money. This is an existential fact. This is the anxiety-provoking guest that, as mentioned, never really leaves any one of us in adult life. In tuning into our children, we can see this and often feel the full intensity of it. In loving our children, many of us might be tempted to shield them from this; or, to restate a phrase from the first chapter of this work, we might be tempted to pay most any sum to the gods to ensure that this decade of their twenties is a fruitful one. However, we know we can't forever shield them from this. The journey is theirs. The long and winding road to individuation commands that it be so.

Time now to rejoin Caitlin. Her world is going to look a little different and her magical love manifesto is going to ring a bit hollow, now that we suspect that she and Dorothy and Toto haven't really left Kansas. Her Aunt Zoe put it less diplomatically, "Of late, I am no fan of my sister and her husband, and their patently bourgeois, unhelpful sympathies toward Caitlin. They did a beautiful job of raising her and her two brothers. Now relax. Let her figure out a few things on her own. And stop commiserating about how rotten the world is, please. I don't know what's gotten into them." Ah, families do have their own special way of expressing love and brutal honesty, don't they? Tell us how you really feel, Zoe! Of course, Zoe had a point—a point that revealed a lot about Caitlin's quixoticism and her accompanying belief that at least some of the burdens of the Open Road belonged to someone else (like, well, her parents?); because, for the time being, they did.

Listen, I will be honest with you,

I do not offer the old smooth prizes, but offer rough new prizes,

These are the days that must happen to you ...

— WALT WHITMAN

Was Caitlin, at age 29 and getting older by the second, in a swivet about what some folks perceived as her diminishing partner prospects? A late twenty-something reader (female) thought so, and conveyed the following message after reading Caitlin's story: "You know, even though I'm no longer single, I couldn't help but think of my friends back in Chicago. Most all went to great schools and grabbed decent post-college jobs, but most now seem distracted by the 'romance gap.' It's almost as if they're putting on hold elements of their personal and professional journey until they pin down the long-term relationship thing. They're all 28 or 29 and kind of panicking." I was caught off guard by this commentary. I thought this pressure had diminished greatly in the modern era. Or, was I woefully out of touch? Now it's true, this is no relevant sample size, and may be unique to that circle of friends. Then again, it may mirror gender pressures that for too many remain alive and well.

Brushing aside these concerns was Caitlin's aunt, the irrepressible Zoe, who at the time of our most recent get-together was carrying her purse like a tomahawk. "I think most days Caitlin, on her own, is fine. She's a fun kid and a real pistol and there's no shortage of eligible bachelors lining up to go out with her. On the other hand, her mother—my dear sister—well, she's the one that's priming the freak-out pump. Of the three kids, Caitlin's the one she loves to worry about. Maybe it's because she's the only girl. Probably. And Bart is no help. He just stands there and shrugs his shoulders, as if that's supposed to mean something. It doesn't. And, I confess, I'm on the warpath because this is crunch time for Caitlin—it's time for her to once and for all take responsibility for her life. In case you don't remember, I haven't always been psycho-over-involved. The last trip she did, whenever that was, about four or five years ago, also Down Under—I was thrilled for her to do something outside the box. But this time around—this jag about her magical love manifesto and going halfway round the world (again!) to find some marrying dude—no, that's weak. The problem isn't love and the answer isn't love. Caitlin's only half a person. That's the problem. Living at home when you're saving for something is one thing. Living at home when you're 32 or 33, which is where she's headed, stuck in the same old life rut and spinning fantasies that are downright deranged, that make no sense whatsoever—and, no, I won't be polite about that in regards to my niece or my sister or my brother-in-law."

. . . .

Rather than continue on where the buffaloes roam and the tomahawks will assuredly fly, I think it wise to stick to the script and say a few final words on Caitlin and the five Agendas of the Open Road, and then, after that, to find a safe perch from where we'll consider how depth of love, missing counterweights and counterbalances in the family system, can work at cross-purposes to Caitlin's task of separation and individuation. Here now the updated notes on Caitlin.

Autonomy (Economic): In a four-years-plus economic holding pattern of residing in her parents' home (rent free), Caitlin eschewed saving in favor of spending money on nice clothes, fun travel, and nights out on the town with her foodie friends. Nothing in and of itself was crazy, though it all added up. A quick rundown of her finances went like this. Each month her checking/debit card account got as low as $200, though never a check did she bounce. This was good. There also was a monthly payment for a quality used car she'd purchased a couple of years back. Her parents had gifted her $5k for the down payment, and she borrowed the rest, about 15k from the credit union, which over 60 months was about $300/month. Perhaps this purchase had been a bit rich for her, but no one had thought that through with her. On the income side, Caitlin had gigged at the local arts center, grossing about $3,200 per month and, taking home (after taxes) approx. $2,400. The quick tally of committed expenses (food/utilities contribution to house kitty $400/month, car payment $300/month, car insurance and gas $200/month, zero per month for rent, zero for medical insurance, and zero per month to savings) left her with $1,500 per month to spend as she wished; and evidently she did just that. On the slightly positive side, since her last major trip five years ago, Caitlin had not raided the cookie jar that consisted of a few blue-chip stock funds in a brokerage account gifted by her grandma and totaling about $40k. During that period, as noted, no additional savings had transpired, either.

Autonomy (Psychological): To borrow a phrase that was fashionable in family therapy circles in the 1980s and 90s, this family system was enmeshed. The damning detail was not that Caitlin lived at home. That could be shaped to a positive or negative outcome. Neither was the main cause over-attunement. Indeed, Caitlin's parents had done that to an excessive degree, a habit very easy to fall into when relating with The Kid We Worry About, which Caitlin most definitely was. Still, that was a lesser issue, and certainly fixable. Instead, the chief cause of the Dread Enmeshment was a particularly insidious mindset—one born of a potent mix of love and fear, one that unified parents and young person *against* the harshness and injustices that occur on the capital side of the Open Road journey.

The appearance of this love-and-fear mindset is understandable, and fully human. On the positive side, and this is a huge positive, the love-and-fear mindset can only arise because there has been an abundance of love. On the negative side, however, this fear-infused love can push some of us, like Caitlin's parents, to make the exactly perfect *wrong* move. This is to say, in such instances we *should* be resolved to mute our own heart's desire to automatically shield and/or comfort the young people, and instead turn the energy and activity toward that of sharpening the sword of critical analysis. This is not easy to do. It is not easy to betray the wishes, if not commands, of one's emotions. It is not easy to see the kids struggle alone. But sometimes it is essential for us to turn and look away. Yes, I know I've been encouraging moments of fearless engagement on our part. Now I'm also encouraging moments of fearless disengagement.

Mom and Dad agreeing that Caitlin's new boss was a Weasel or a Turkey or a Bad Person, did little for Caitlin. Yes, she'd been nicked and bruised, and it was up to her lick her own wounds. And there was no time to waste. Forget about love: The capital clock was ticking. She had a decision to make: Would she dwell in upset and fly away to New Zealand, or get back out there and see this agenda through? If yes to the latter, then what was the plan? Now that's for Caitlin and her people to rally round.

Family: Caitlin was entangled in a goopy bourgeois worldview that she couldn't help but share with her parents. To her mom in particular, the capital side of life seemed unduly harsh for her little girl. No disagreement from me on the critique of capitalism in 21st-century America, but how did this fundamental perspective empower Caitlin? It didn't. In fact, it pushed her to bouts of wild reverie, the recurring theme being how to bypass the capital side of life—which was starting to resemble a beast. Of course, marrying some dude who would slay the capital beast is hardly a new concept. And regardless of the happy ending that Caitlin envisioned for herself in her magical love manifesto, I saw trouble. Marrying such a dude was hardly the road to personal or financial freedom.

Henceforward, I think it's going to be quite the task for Caitlin to sort all this out. I hope to heck she does. Her aunt is a tremendous resource, but the sway of parents will remain most powerful. If I had my fantasy moment with Caitlin's parents, I'd nudge them to acknowledge where the most important power lies; namely, in their daughter. I don't think they see that or believe in that. To wit, keeping their daughter "untested" in many ways confirms this view of Caitlin as not having the power to learn and grow and meet the demands of the capital side of life. It goes one step further, this fantasy moment of mine. I would summon the words of Whitman here. The sublime goal isn't just that we teach the young people to embrace the difficulties and obstacles of the journey, but, indeed, to go one step further and transform them into delicious burdens.

Adventure: Once upon a time the notion that adventure and love would dispel the considerable challenges posed to Caitlin by the agenda of autonomy—well, that had been quaint and cute and charming and, yes, quixotic. It had almost worked. There's no gainsaying Adam Smith and Karl Marx got restless in their graves as she did almost rearrange the fabric of the universe. But, as Groucho liked to say: Close, but no cigar! And now, this All World Quixotic Move of hers is becoming odd. The "capital clock" ticks and the ordering of things increasingly matters. *Get the job, make the life that allows the adventure; not the other way around.* Time to make some serious decisions about the capital side of life, and commit to them, or else she might find herself painted into a corner.

Romantic Love: Other than to reiterate the opinion that two *whole* people coming together is a brighter and more auspicious approach to love and long-term committed relationship, I have nothing further to say.

Passion/Gift: Had Caitlin's work in the arts community expressed her personal gifts/passions/talents in some meaningful way? Hard to say. Caitlin had always carried herself with such dramatic flair that it seemed natural to assume she was right where she wanted to be. But the last time I saw her she looked lost.

· · · · · · · ·

After hunkering down in her work and proving herself very capable in the arts/educational not-for-profit world these past four years, Caitlin hit a wall. Her old boss, the very winning Executive Director (ED), had left the organization for family reasons, but the transition hadn't gone too well. The New ED arrived chock full of her own ideas but evidently wasn't interested in Caitlin's input. In such a small organization, this was awkward. Caitlin attempted to broach the matter, but her boss said every-thing between them was "peachy." Feeling slightly desperate, Caitlin responded by rolling the dice and asking for a raise. I don't know how exactly she came up with that idea, but the New ED ignored the request. This was not good. We know what Caitlin did from here. One, she gave notice. Two, she hatched the idea of the New Zealand trip. Three, she gathered data on the mythic island, spending hours on the web scrolling through pics of land and sea and, most ardently, the people. Caitlin decided that he must be in there somewhere amongst them. *Definitely an Auck-lander. Rugby player, or horseman? Not sure. Might be literary! Must be a handsome devil at any rate!* Okay, I've embellished here. Bringing it back, I pass along the analysis of Zoe, her aunt and best friend. She felt that, beneath Caitlin's breezy assertions that her resignation didn't matter, Caitlin's world had seriously been rocked by this change of bosses and she'd gotten frustrated and depressed, and, in the end, acted rashly. Zoe also admitted blow-ing her stack at Caitlin upon learning that she'd quit her job. "She should have talked to me, or somebody. Anybody! This was the moment when you make lemonade out of lemons. The girl had options in the not-for-profit world. But she instead decided to dive into a pocket of low self-esteem and self-pity and throw away all the good things she had created for herself at the arts center."

It had been shortly after this fiery encounter with Zoe that Caitlin called and had the quasi-contritional tea with me.

Detour from the Agenda of Autonomy

Zoe clearly saw what some of us would have recognized: Caitlin quit at the exact moment when she needed to lean into the situation and develop some strategy and garner emotional support. Yes, the situation had been very difficult. Caitlin had felt frustrated, and understandably so. What had been a lively and endlessly interesting place to work now became dreary as dreary could be. It wasn't fair, but this was no time to lament about unfairness. Caitlin had had options. People in the community knew her and appreciated her excellent work these past four years. Such social assets were real, though they didn't necessarily make the challenges before her any easier. But Caitlin checked out. She took a detour headed in a peculiar direction, one that went as far as is imaginable from securing economic autonomy, one that dramatically reduced the work/career value she'd been creating. The latter was what Zoe found so maddening. For, this had been the moment for Caitlin to be resilient and resourceful.

It was tough to see a young person lose patience in the face of very real external obstacles, especially when she was this deep into building for herself a solid career foundation. For many a good kid, this part of the journey takes time and cannot be rushed. I myself think the *career arc (money included)* takes anywhere from 6 to 10 years to hit something resembling cruising altitude. Ordinary are the assortment of headwinds and bumps, and revised flight plans, before most kids stabilize their work situation *and* get paid adequately, or better, for it. Regarding the plight of Caitlin, in an alternative world she'd have kept at her job and, with a little help from her friends, put the word out and systematically created some new options for herself. It was, as her Aunt Zoe had noted, the moment to figure out how to make lemonade out of life's lemons, and definitely not the moment to "switch out" by making exotic plans infused with all sorts of fanciful hopes and dreams. But what's done is done. And, in regards to the task of economic autonomy, Caitlin now has put herself in a difficult spot, made no easier by the fact that she is fast approaching the age of 30 when, quite reliably, the open road tends to narrow. Even so, perhaps her penchant for charm and luck will ultimately win the day. Better, perhaps she'll bounce back quicker than expected, maybe even forego all of this New Zealand nonsense. Only time will tell.

Chapter 16 Art of Betrayal

I propose one final cognitive challenge to the parents of the Kids We Worry About.

Can you, from time to time, choose to look the other way? Can you, on occasion, decide to tune out? It won't be easy. Separation and individuation involve a bit of betrayal by both parties … the good sort of betrayal … kind of like when you find out your good friends have other friends you didn't know about, or vice versa: *I didn't know you chill with Ariella and Tariq!* Everyday life is full of small and necessary betrayals. This is healthy.

Put differently, and apropos the KWWA matter at hand: What if there is some existing dynamic, the source of which is a Genuine Mystery, and that existing dynamic ensures that your kid will do things that make you worry? If so, can you disown what's going on? Can you look in a different direction? Or—and this is probably highly unlikely—can you look directly at the Kid You Worry About in that moment and affirm the undeniable fact that she is her own agent, making her own choices, and it's time for you to cut through your thinking mind?

It won't be easy. The Kids We Worry About are most likely to be the twentysomethings who live at home for vast stretches of time. As such, they'll perform their nerve-wracking acts right in front of us. A thought, then: These are exactly the kids who need to live elsewhere ... because we need to not witness this all the time. Crazy? You bet it's crazy.

The idea is to somehow interrupt the constant inter-looping of nervous systems. The fear-infused-love is contagious. Our kid's fear is contagious. Thus I offer you an idea. Consider the art of betrayal. That is, love them all the time, but only tune in some of the time. Then, there's the much more difficult task—figuring out what to do with those free and open spaces in your mind and your life. No kidding.

Allons! Whoever you are, come travel with me!

Traveling with me you find what never tires.

The earth never tires,

The earth is rude, silent, incomprehensible at first,

Nature is rude

and incomprehensible at first,

Be not discouraged, keep on, there are divine things enveloped,

I swear to you there are divine things

more beautiful than words can tell.

— WALT WHITMAN

Chapter 17 # Rude

As expressed at the outset, yes, it is true, I was once a tiny pumpkin, growing on a pumpkin vine. And that included the riot incited by me when I was 25 and signed an apartment lease before I got the job, and Maria was looking very pregnant then, and my father-in-law wasn't amused and he got all sword-wieldy, and, yes, blood spurted here and there on the sidewalk of 7th Avenue, my blood, and for a while it was touch and go in the ICU, but, miracle of miracles, I came out of it. Anyway, I'd like to say a few words about my parents and their generation—you know, the tree from which this apple fell—and, then pick up the story of my life in the country with Maria and the kids circa 1993. It was right around that time that the earth stopped being silent and incomprehensible, and it laid something of a rude awakening on me, as per the capital side of me and my family's life.

TREE

In my heart I carry a great love and affection for my parents. My father and I had twelve years together on this earth before he died, but here's the weird thing: I've never felt shortchanged by this. Grieve my father's death? Yes, to this day, some forty years down the line, I grieve that loss. But the brightness of our time together never wanes. I cannot say exactly why, except it undoubtedly helps that we had scores upon scores of good times together, fishing and going to ballgames, and working on local political campaigns, and the family taking trips in the big station wagon all over the place, and the trips to Hunts Point at 3am to pick up produce, and him taking me to the store to work with him on the occasional Saturday. Naturally, I'm prone to embellishment, but that's how I remember my time with him. My mother, fortunately, survived the vicissitudes of my dad's untimely death, and indeed was a rock back then. Heroic in her own way. Tough in her own way. Not easy being a widow at age 36 with four kids and three businesses to run. Perhaps it was a bit of role reversal, but my father had been the nurturing parent for me while my mother proved to be the reliable and savvy warrior in the world.

I also carry a deep loyalty and respect for my in-laws. They, like my mother, doubtless found my journey at times maddening, but fundamentally they were there for Maria and me and the children. I feel genuine appreciation for that. This is not to assert that they or my parents were paragons of perfection in family life. Obviously, that's not possible. But all of them were solid. They ably provided, and sent us to the good schools, and underwrote countless fun times and adventures; and, they made much of that look easy. Perhaps most importantly, they raised the bar for us in our life. There was nothing fuzzy about what was expected of us. That said, when it came to matters of individuation, to the nitty-gritty of what it meant to be true to one's spirit, to take to the open road "leading wherever I choose"—no, that line of communication wasn't up and working. Sure, here and there could be found exceptions to that norm, but mostly the expectations were capital-centric. Given that, I (my younger self) looked around at the adults in my world, and knew I was on my own. Who I was becoming and what I was interested in exploring as I came of age—indeed, given the era, it was a wise decision to keep it to myself and go stealth. I was not alone in wanting to avoid the sting of criticism and judgment. At the end of the day there was no hero's badge to pin on my chest for going solo. It was simply my best strategy in light of the times. And, as we saw, when I forgot to go stealth, the world handed me a healthful, to-the-hilt reminder!

Which reminds me: At the beginning of this essay I waved my pen at the idea of a bigger conversation that—in lieu of 7th Avenue sword waving and slashing—could have gone down between Svend and me. But that wave of mine was without merit. For, it is anachronistic of me to even suggest that Svend missed the opportunity to discuss money matters in the way that we've been doing herein. A more rounded notion of financial education, one that accounts for the complexity of being one's own genuine person in this world, one that addresses matters of money *in the service* of independence, adventure, romantic love, passion/gifts, and family—that rounded notion of financial education simply did not exist back in the day. Sure, lessons were gleaned here and there, and on occasion someone of the older generation generously pointed out how to handle an aspect of money or to negotiate compensation for a summer job, but there was no systematic, ongoing conversation between the generations. Nor was there an identified need. I have long had the sense that many of my parents' generation considered the tasks and competencies associated with money to be self-evident. "You choose to be competent or you choose to be a ne'er-do-well."

Absence of dialogue between generations had other antecedents, too. In many families and social circles, the topic of money was regarded as crass. Off-putting. More taboo than sex, as Freud once wrote. You could talk biz in some families, like mine, but never personal money. I remember being ten years old and coming home from a playdate where my friend had accusingly said, "Your family's rich," and I'd felt embarrassed about the whole thing; so I asked my mom (when I got home) if we were rich, and she said, "No, we're middle class," and then gave me the stern smile that meant, This conversation is over, now go and do your homework. Well, that institution of taboo and weirdness is crumbling, thank goodness. So many of us now acknowledge that a rounded financial education is comprised of scores upon scores of conversations with our kid. Arduous? Yes. Essential? Yes. Devil in the details kind of thing? For sure. Fulfilling? Should be some of the most rewarding discussions we have with them.

LIFE IN THE COUNTRY – C. 1993

As to the path of my younger self, returning to the bucolic scene of living in Woodstock with my pregnant sweetheart in the winter of '88, I did land a pretty good job in the mental health field that easily covered the monthly nut. It got better. A short year later I began what would become a multi-year gig with a family therapy organization in Kingston, the central city of Ulster County. There, I trained in the ways and means of family therapy. I found this work incredibly stimulating. The other therapists on the team were cool. All of us trained old school in front of a one-way mirror, the rest of the team behind it, critiquing the work and at times intervening mid-session. The paycheck itself was decent (yep, we could get by on 28k per year from me and 12k from Maria teaching part-time). And that is how life went. It took us on a ride that was wholly unplanned. Life was good, despite the future consistently being opaque. Could not see two years out. Could not see twenty years out. What young person ever can?

But I didn't know this then. I didn't fully recognize the limitation of no visibility and no game plan. Nor was I fully engaged on the capital side. In its place I had my own rendition of magical thinking. To this day, I admit, I still adhere to vestiges, but the part that had to do with attempting to bypass portions of the capital side of life—well, I'll say I'm inclined to admire those who try their hand at various forms of magical thinking, but up to a point. For me and for Caitlin that point was the age of 30. There's nothing particularly sacred or hard about that moment in time. Rather, the start of this new decade predictably brings with it various *ripenings* and *reckonings*. Those Open Road agendas which have been well-tended to, often start to yield good fruit. Those which are still in the state of becoming, like Caitlin's work life, call for renewed commitment and moxie. And, that which has been neglected, whether several agendas or one, will predictably have a way of returning—and returning in force. This last one will likely not be fun, and may well disrupt activity in the other domains. In the case of my younger self, I had not fully turned my mind to one ... no, actually, *less* than one agenda ... a mere one half of one agenda, to which I had theretofore given an 80% effort! I say *mere* and *80%* as if that would make me eligible for an Open Road dispensation. And, why not? I mean, Sheesh! Wasn't 4.5 out of the 5 agendas in hand at least deserving of an honorable mention?

No, actually, it was not.

But that can't be right.

Let's again look at my scorecard.

Romantic love knocked on my door and I was 22. Seemed great to me, and it was. Check. Family and children snuck in the side door three years later. I loved family life immediately. Check. My deep passion and keen interest for matters of spirit and psyche took me off the beaten path, sending me to the buddhist-inspired Naropa University instead of law school. Not an ounce of disappointment or regret there. Check. In regards to adventure, I felt the bounty of experiences linked to love, family, Naropa and later living in the country. This basket of experiences felt plenty adventurous to me. Check. So, 4.5 out of 5 looked pretty good, except, well, yes, in my blind spot still lurked the capital side of autonomy. More to the point, I had miscalculated what was needed on the capital side of *family autonomy*.

The rude awakening occurred in the late spring of 1993. Colliding with an otherwise lovely Hudson Valley existence was the fast approaching future of not me, not Maria, but our children. One year thence our oldest child, Mikyo, would enter first grade. His little sister, several years behind, would follow suit. You could say we had officially entered the "time flies" vortex of family life, and the problem of primary education had seemingly come out of nowhere—except we had been subtly and quite successfully ignoring it, too. For Maria and me, there was no philosophical rift. We had always shared the view of education-as-religion. But imputing the economics and the geography of it was another matter. We were underwhelmed by what we knew of the local public school. Unfortunately, we had failed to consciously put that on the table of economic problems to be solved. And now here it was, fast approaching. Whether moving to a school district with the super good schools or sending the kids to private day school, those options would cost money. Maybe even a lot of money. It made my head spin. Striking out on this education piece for the children was simply unacceptable. Covering the costs of private education on 40k per year household income wasn't going to cut it. I had to do something. But, what?

. . . .

There was no inkling that down the road of life my family therapy training would prove fortuitous and practical. Not that today I, as financial advisor and money manager, do anything remotely resembling therapy. I don't! But since mine is a business that frequently deals with large emotions (i.e., around money, lifestyle, spending, planning, and smartly supporting the young people), and since mine is a business that frequently works to dissuade folks from counterproductive investor behaviors/decision-making, I think the training ends up being spot on. Who knew the capital value of a Naropa education? Not I. Nor would I, until the decade of my forties when I gained the years-on perspective to connect the dots on this truth.

However, mine was not all a story of photos of toothy smiles atop mountain peaks.

Deep and angsty were the valleys between leaving the not-for-profit psychotherapy world, going to work for a large investment brokerage firm and then finally launching my own business. It would take seven years before I relaxed and felt confident that my company would survive, and another four to economically thrive. Remember the old maxim of how it takes three years to launch a business? Tosh, I say. That's nuts. I think folks now know the norm is indeed closer to seven years, at least in my line of work. So, the early years on a new track (and in a new town, back in Boulder) were brutal. Launching my financial advisory business under the umbrella of American Express had its advantages in the marketplace, and the training was cool and promising and already proving to be a curiously suitable follow-on to my psychotherapy work. Still, it was tough. Getting that first batch of new clients was frighteningly difficult. Although I knew I was now on the right capital track, the initial stipend provided by Amex for a budding advisor was modest and I felt so financially stressed out that there were days when I ditched my co-workers and ate lunch by myself in my old Saab and cried. I was scared and totally out of control and fearing that we might crash and all four of us have to head back to New York and take up residence in the third floor of my in-laws' house. Our oldest child had begun first grade at a private school in Boulder, and we were paying a tuition that at that particular moment we had no business doing. We were leaking oil at an alarming rate and I didn't have the guts to say so to my wife. For her part, she was ignoring the situation with pinpoint accuracy: She was super busy in her role as stay-at-home mom, and knew just where *not* to look. But the crux of the matter was that the launch of my financial advisory practice was taking longer than I had imagined. On the one side I was under-capitalized. On the other I was spending when I should have been tight-fisted.

What gave?

I summoned counsel and financial support from every available quarter is what gave. Talk about embarrassing. Except there was no time to be embarrassed. In my mind were visions of the third floor of my father-in-law, Svend's, house. Talk about motivation! My godson Spencer needed to wait tables *ad nauseam* and sleep in his dad's woodworking shop, but I think my negative motivation took the cake. In Part Two I circumambulate the topic of what all goes into "the launch" of the kids in the decade of their twenties. One theme concerns *flying economically low,* of which there are various, shall we say, expressions. As for my younger self, having made an ambitious change in my professional life, and having done so late in the game and with fewer arrows in my quiver than I should have had, I can say with true humility that I flew lower that I ever wish to see anyone else fly. I touched the tops of trees, and it all still makes my heart skip a beat just to think about it. Which doesn't mean I won't let my own kids fly that low, or crash, if that's what they need to do, or if that's what they're hell bent on doing. I shan't say too much more, saving that for Part Two, but what I will say is that I don't think those angsty years in the valley were caused by some adolescent pathology. Something was missing. No, I'm not going to cut to the scene where the bad guy in the movie, right before he dies, says that society made him do it! I own my journey. But I also see that a critical piece was missing, to wit, a game plan. And as such I posit a rather social idea about remedies: Namely, if we do but one thing with our twentysomethings, it's to gently and consistently and firmly convey the idea that they need a game plan. Their own game plan. Timeline on this: By the end of their twenty-something decade.

Allons! to that which is endless as it was beginningless

To undergo much, tramps of day, rests of nights,

To merge all in the travel they tend to, and the days and nights

they tend to,

Again to merge them in the start of superior journeys ...

— WALT WHITMAN

 Up Around the Bend

Left to my own devices, I did not, until my early thirties, begin in earnest this inquiry of self, world, and of course money. And who, pray tell, was the guru that set this inquiry upon me? Answer: The Phenomenal World care of Its Tremendously Accurate Feedback. Up till then my modest successes—i.e., being good at getting decent jobs that paid crap but had good benefits—simply served to forestall the inevitable. And then the inevitable hit me. My miscalculations and missing data about myself, business, the economics of family life, and the world, crashed on my back like a succession of cold massive ocean waves. I did not see it coming, but then it was all I saw. So, I can't really tell you that my semi-enlightened intuitive side sweetly turned my mind to the money thing. Rather, that spot-on Phenomenal World jolted me into awakening with a rush of adrenaline and then some.

No surprise that my children coming of age, along with this book project, prompted me to contemplate the all of it—the good, the bad, the joyous, the edgy, as well as how the times have changed and, in particular, how the dialogue between the generations has been upgraded. There are pieces in this essay that are repackaged notions from my upbringing, care of my parents who came of age in the 1950s. I'm glad they raised the bar for me in certain ways, even if it took me a long time to sort through what I wanted to keep and what I wanted to take a pass on. There also are pieces in this inquiry that leave those sensibilities far behind, the foremost being the low value placed on the process of individuation. *Be your own person in this world. Be your own person. Figure that out, but figure it out—money included.* Maria and I ventured in this direction of individuation-as-supreme a little bit before our time. This meant we had to steal past various threshold guardians, but that also left us prone to being secretive and careful about those from whom we sought vision and counsel. It was what it was. I made some good mistakes and some bad mistakes, and while most make me smile, a few make me groan. Sometimes the most fruitful reflections in life come, not from the victories, but from the defeats. And that is the lead-in to one final idea, as ordinary as oatmeal in the morning, and, it is hoped, as nourishing.

Yep, Thinking about Us in the Critical Role of Savvy Planner Friend

Planning is one of those dreadfully bland words. I myself hear the word and fear I might fall asleep in the hills like good old Rip, only to awaken 20 years later. That said, I should show the word more respect because, until age 30, it's what was missing in my journey. I lacked a plan, a *dynamic plan.* My life vision was good and idealistic. However, my life vision, *money included,* was fraught with blind spots and questionable assumptions—assumptions that definitely needed to be questioned. Instead, I had my experiment with magical thinking going on. At the time it seemed to me that a virtuous person should be luckier and thus able to "magnetize" capital in an array of unorthodox (i.e., non-capital) ways. My hypothesis was that virtue should invoke its own kind of magic. Looking back, I don't think I was wholly wrong, but more analysis and less faith would have been beneficial. Secondly, there were my skills around money. On default mode, I assumed said skills were pretty good. Did I stop to evaluate where I was sharp and where I wasn't? Did I take proper stock of my earnings power and opportunities? No, I did not. That, too, would have been useful. But, without letting myself off the hook, I nonetheless think it fair to say that something essential was missing—a vital element that by myself I would never have mustered:

Visibility.

Allow me to wipe my glasses, tie my shoes, and unpack this a bit.

This phenomenon, namely, lack of visibility, seems part and parcel of the decade of one's twenties, and it makes effective planning by one's lonesome near impossible. It is easy to forget this fact. The road indeed opens before the young people, presenting them with all manner of mundane and exotic choices, but that doesn't mean they can see where their decisions will lead them. Not by themselves, anyway. Why this occurs is anyone's guess. Nevertheless, there it is. For most any twenty-something person, it is so hard to see one, two, or five years out. This was true for me. I wasn't being derelict in my parental duties. It's just that the economics of family and in particular educating my children had never fully dawned in my mind until there it was, standing right in front of Maria and me, our oldest kid's first-grade year but twelve months away. Did I need a game plan? You bet I did. I needed a game plan in the overarching sense, in the detailed sense, and it also needed to resonate with me on a deeply personal level.

Nowadays, this is easily remedied.

The antidote to this lack of visibility comes from the warming and clarifying sun of *relationships*. The young people, by themselves, can't know what they don't know. More, it is exceedingly difficult for them to recognize the extent to which they can't see very far in front of them. The pervasive cultural myth of uber-individualism only further confuses the matter. It says: *In order to be true individuals, the young people need to figure everything out by themselves.* This is absurd. This is how the wrong kind of mistakes get made. The bad mistakes. The mistakes that don't generate insight or growth, but make a big fat mess. Therefore, the task here for the young people leads the other way; not inward, not isolation-ward, nor by oneself making wild guesses or making stuff up, but by going outward, to the realm of relationships, where they can get useful sounding-boards and feedback and data and perspective. This is powerful. This is how they can shine a light on the otherwise opaque passages of the journey. Indeed, when the kids make it a point to "gather their people" and engage them, this should be regarded as a very willful and powerful expression of taking personal responsibility for their life. Now the idea of having a game plan is actually realizable.

Still and all, how will the young people know to gather and engage their people? Actually, without us, they won't. So, enlightening them is the first job of the guide-as-savvy-planner-friend. For as long as it takes, we must challenge them to acknowledge this principal fact of twenty-something life. You need a game plan on the one hand. On the other hand, visibility is low on the open road. Blind spots abound. There's no reason to feel bad about it. But don't linger in that state either. *Gather (and use) your people.* In the course of this work I maintain that this is the one and only rule of the Open Road. I very much hope you will buy into this view. Not only is it a practical and useful mode of journeying for the kids, a kind of social Swiss army knife, but it helps an awful lot when we need to step back or just let go. On more than one occasion it has served that sword-like purpose: *Then I trust you are discussing this with your people ...* (after which I really do shut my mouth).

Of course, we are our kids' first people! As parents, aunts/uncles, et al, we have occupied the role of savvy planner friend from the get-go. But, as the kids get older and stronger in their being, they will increasingly take control of whom they activate and when. That seems wholly appropriate. Yet, we need not be shy. It's fine to assert that we know a thing or two about being a savvy planner friend. This might mean that there are moments when we mind their business. It's also fine for us to dream dreams of who we sense our kids might really be. It won't hurt them. It won't make them passive. It won't make them beholden. Quite the opposite. Most of them know full well they can push back, and do so without big repercussions. The young people might even welcome our proactive engagement: *What about this detail? Have you thought about that likely outcome? Have you thought about it deeply? Are you discussing a, b, or c plans, if not with me, then with "your people?" Would you like to discuss it with me? Are you aware that you're not addressing this agenda over here?*

. . . .

Not that one can turn back the clock, nor is that even desirable, but from time to time I do enjoy the "what if things had played differently" parlor game. In this instance, as per me and my living-in-the-country younger self, I suspect that just about any topic could have been advanced *if* I had felt that warm, Whitman-esque openness from the adults around me: "So, Mark, you went to Naropa, and now you're living in the country and you've got a young family, and you guys are doing the buddhist thing. Okay, cool. But now what? What is your vision for buying a home? You don't want to be a renter forever, do you? What is your vision for educating your children? Educating them ain't free ... not even public school is free! What is your vision for work? Does living in this country environment afford you the opportunities you may want and/or need? By the way, I heard you went to Naropa instead of law school. Have you considered going to law school now? What about that work/family/time/money configuration? How will you and Maria juggle all of this? What have you tried? What worked, what did not work? On a more practical note, are you saving?"

While I did not have that savvy planner friend in my life back then, I did make a strong and lasting connection with a gentle-man who fit 87.5% of that description; he was a truly savvy if not sagacious person. Twenty-five years my senior, Joachim beamed Whitmanesque rays of warmth on me and my young family. This was tremendously nourishing. All topics were up for discussion and indeed we discussed everything—art, politics, writing, dhar-ma, family, and shamanism. Interestingly, and certainly through no fault of his own, or mine for that matter, we never touched the subject of money. Never touched on how money ran in and through most all of these streams of life and love and being in this world. Kind of amazing, this omission. And yet it was not amaz-ing! People share blind spots all the time. Good people. Or maybe it was that talking about money was too awkward, or too socially risky, or simply not what was in the air in the early 1990s—and of course Joachim had grown up in the 1950s. In any case, this capital koan of the open road, unceremoniously delivered to the doorstep of my sweet country home when I was 30 years old, set me to thinking. I sought answers. I sharpened questions. To this day I remain fascinated by one particular basket of questions: *How might deeply creative and spiritual people make their way in this decidedly capital country? What does it take? What are the trade-offs? Who do they need around them? What kind of support, and when? How much worldly power does a GDI or bodhisattva need to be relevant and effective—today, now, here?*

On this capital inquiry I have made the thousand notes to self. Amid the mélange of experiential victories and defeats in my own life, I have gone back and revised these notes. In my role as friend and advisor to some really fine people, I have further witnessed what has worked and failed to work for them, and thusly imputed. All of it plays. All of it is worth combing through. None of it should be rejected. The moment we as guides speak from our total experience, merging hard-won insights to honest dogged bewilderments, something truly magical happens. Our offering becomes treasure. Not perfect treasure, mind you. Some of it has the mud of confusion all over it. But it doesn't matter. Confusion doesn't disqualify us. Dishonesty disqualifies us. Bloviating disqualifies us. But, no, confusion is a part of the rich and fertile offering of ideas, stories, and honest questions we put out there to our kid. There are many ways to occupy the role of Savvy Planner Friend, but my point is we don't need to be all tidy and together about it. Life certainly isn't all tidy. But enough of my musings, let's turn and head, if not for home, then for the high country where the earth remains rude, the continent indeed divides, and the streams swell and then in late summer run dry.

Henceforth I ask not good-fortune, I myself am good-fortune,
Henceforth I whimper no more, postpone no more, need nothing,
Done with indoor complaints, libraries, querulous criticisms,
Strong and content I travel the open road.

— WALT WHITMAN

 # The True Wealth
of this Great Nation

I know the world needs a lot of healing and mending, less violence and more kindness and laughter. Even so, I think our children are coming of age in an auspicious time and place. The culturally acknowledged importance of their *selfhood* is a very recent social development. By contrast, in 1988, when I signed a lease for an apartment in Woodstock, New York (before being gainfully employed), I got put in the penalty box for using a logic that was decidedly non-capital. And although it was not well received, it could have been worse. The Almost Whole Truth is, my then pregnant wife, Maria, and I wanted to live there so as to be near the Tibetan Buddhist monastery and the Zen monastery. Gluttons for meditative punishment? No doubt. The stuff of treasonous rebellion? No, I don't think so. A pushback against excessive materialism? In a way. Genuine interest in the dharma, meditation, and life in the country? To be sure. But we never remotely considered sharing this premier fact with the older generation. Our parents would have been deeply distressed.

No real surprises here, when I think about how our parents came of age. 1950s white middle/upper-middle class America was intense. It was a time to make hay. The rules of society and race and gender were strict, and solid, and stern. There were only the faintest of murmurs of the much needed social and moral revolutions that the 1960s would usher in. Our parents were indeed parents themselves by then! But back in their coming of age time, the highly scripted dreams of 1950s heroism had been decidedly extraverted. Punch a wise guy in the eye. Send a man to the moon. Make a million bucks. And proceed in a capital-first manner. That was the zeitgeist. What had my father deep down wanted to be or to do in his all-too-short life? What might my father-in-law have pursued, had he rebelled and taken to the open road? I can't open that box. The anachronisms keep it locked shut. With the exception of lunatic (!) poets and writers like Kerouac and Ginsberg, no one born into that socioeconomic time and place wanted to get put in the counterculture penalty box. It really was to be avoided at all costs. It should come as no surprise to us, then, that matters of soul and selfhood, of spirit and authenticity, of earth and sun—were often neglected, overlooked, discounted, if not perceived as the enemy.

With all of that still bouncing around as I came of age, I learned to stick to the exteriors of the journey. Dress nicely. Keep good company. Be polite. Attend university. Work hard. Be conscientious in my dealings. And I did see the virtues in this social training. It's just that so much was not up for discussion. Perhaps for most of my friends that was no big deal. But as I reeled during my teen years from the untimely death of my father, I felt like my whole being was on fire. I took to the open road the first chance I got. And as I made my way, I would like to tell you how I forthwith sought out thought-partners and mentors and guides. But, no, it took a while for me to figure out whom to trust. I had learned stealth and I had learned that one misplay and you could find yourself in a bad way. No matter. Good fortune became me. I found my people. One here, one there. I could name names. I could draw faces. Good folks, very generous in giving of themselves. Each and every one encouraging me to be myself. Such a debt of gratitude do I feel—in many ways the impetus of this work.

SONG OF TOMORROW

By leaps and bounds, the times have changed. Authenticity is manna. The Open Road holds the possibilities of the world and the possibilities of the psyche. To be authentic, I posit, is to be good fortune. The parents of this time and place are extraordinary, moreover. So many are attuned to and support this ambitious undertaking of selfhood by the young people. I look around, and this seems increasingly normative. And deep. And socially promising. And promising for the planet:

> *Now I see the secret of the making of the best persons,*
> *It is to grow in the open air, and to eat and sleep with the earth.*
>
> *Here a great personal deed has room,*
> *(A great deed seizes upon the hearts of the whole race of men,*
> *Its effusion of strength and will overwhelms law,*
> *   and mocks all authority and all argument against it.)*

> — WALT WHITMAN

I feel tremendous confidence in who our young people are. They look, to my eye, like the stuff of old and wise souls. Activism seems to be woven into their DNA, into who they are and how they move through the world. Of course, they have much to learn, and the tests of the fast-approaching future will be all their own. Still, I sense there is something heroic about them. For me, this is an unlikely choice of words, since, until very recently, I steered clear of the term "hero." And then, quite wonderfully, Life served up on a silver platter (okay, it was on the screen of an Apple computer) the answer to a question I had yet to ask. I was watching a replay from the 1993 Joseph Campbell interviews by Bill Moyers on PBS, and there it was bright and shiny in Campbell's reply to the query about how the hero might look or act today: He said, "The influence of a vital person ... *vitalizes*. This is what a hero does." Well, no doubt, this is true. When people are vital in their life, something magical yet ordinary does indeed vitalize others, if not the environment. Lawyers can be great change agents, fight noble causes, renew our belief in justice; or, they can be soulless life-depleting mercenaries. Mothers and fathers can create the space for sane and grounded individuals (their kids!) to day-in day-out learn and grow and thus feel the goodness of becoming themselves; or, parents can sow the seeds of strife and discontent in the ground of their children's being. Bankers can turn capital markets on their head, perhaps even usher in what would be a truly fascinating (and much desired) Capitalism 3.0; or, they can revert to their asininely greedy ways. Artists can heal through joy and beauty, through vibrations and rhythm; or, they can be so mired in economic distractions that they never get to offer up their particular brand of social medicine. In pith, great bodhisattvas come in all shapes and sizes, don all manner of costumes, and converse in both cockney and the Queen's English. And, great bodhisattvas have resonance. All of them have resonance, and creativity, and whatever stuff goes into bringing the extremes, human and planetary, back into balance. I speak of the resonance and vitality born of authenticity. I speak of the resonance and vitality born of fresh vision. And, in singing all of this, I'm thinking of the young people—the true wealth of our nation, upon whom the future of so much depends.

MID-AMBLE

It wasn't a matter that I followed closely, this pushing and shoving between so-called hands-off parents and over-involved parents, mostly because it didn't hit close to home. I don't mean to sound condescending. We in Boulder have our own assortment of social frictions, to be sure, but this isn't one of them. My information thus came by way of references in the *New York Times* and from my friends in Rye who every now and again murmured acid words against what they deemed the town's dread helicopter-hovering parental contingent. I've still never seen these parents in action, nor do I care to, but clearly they must be out there roaming the countryside, terrorizing the upper-middle class suburbs with their relentless pursuit of winning (and winning big). Anyway, I thought the micro-aggressions had faded away since I hadn't heard the helicopter parent phrase uttered in a dog's age. And I would still think that way had I let sleeping magazines lie. But, no, I had to crack open a 2016 summer issue of the *Atlantic* that had been ably serving as a coaster, with dried water welts on the now crinkly cover, when there it was, alive and well, emblazoned on the Table of Contents page: "How Helicopter Parents Can Cause

Binge Drinking." To which I thought, *Well, for once I don't have a dog in this fight. Here goes nothing!* The sensationalism of the title notwithstanding, I found it to be an excellent piece, both edifying and substantive. The author, one Caitlin Flanagan (no relation to our Quixotic Caitlin, by the way), presented a cogent critique of a particularly virulent form of parental over-involvement. And the more I read, the more I was struck by how the content of the article offered a stark and rather depressing contrast to what we've been up to with our Open Road inquiry.

Heretofore, when I'd heard the phrase helicopter parenting, I assumed it referred to sweet, compulsive parents who over-managed and over-scheduled and over-strategized their kids' every move, day in and day out. Starring in these roles I pictured lovable, goofy and annoying actors like Steve Martin and Rick Moranis. I did not, however, connect this parenting style to the endgame under indictment in the *Atlantic* article. Therein, Ms. Flanagan presented a picture of two generations working in tandem toward the achievement of very specific, ambitious socioeconomic goals. Get into the top schools, occupy the professions that pay the big bucks, and achieve something akin to the stature of the older generation. Now, I want to tread carefully here. I don't mean to imply that all kids, or even the majority of kids, at the nation's top schools are there because their parents sat on their heads since the age of 12 or 13. I also want to recognize the fine line that can exist between parents being consistently encouraging and parents being too directive. And the open road doesn't make clarifying this line any easier. In a number of professions, the prep and then actual launch take a long time and require tremendous sustained effort. Family support for any kid to get into and then through medical school, for example, is a seeming necessity these days. But Ms. Flanagan had something else in mind. In some quarters of upper-middle class America, things in the parent/child partnership had evidently gone too far. Or had they? Hard to argue with success, except the kids' wildly dangerous behaviors were clearly signaling something else. No doubt predicated on love but also on some manner of family narcissism, this extreme parental approach to coming-of-age challenges was taking its toll on the plethora of young people.

Which brings us back to Ms. Flanagan's stinging critique. The path that one-pointedly seeks overt power and its tributes is characterized by extremes that can innocently or perhaps intentionally leap over matters of character development, spirit, and authenticity. Those extremes can also beget a slew of destructive behaviors, the damage of which goes in a number of directions, binge-drinking being one of them. Now call me naïve, but I found this dark side of helicopter parenting to be news. And at the risk of being painfully unsubtle, I add this aspiration: In the course of our kids' Open Road journey and in the totality of their life, may they generate sufficient capital strength, autonomy, and canniness so that they're never in subordinate positions to such persons bred in this toxic manner. Idealistic aspiration on my part? Maybe. Except I'd like to kick it out further. May our kids one day be in the position to dethrone this deeply misguided lot that too often occupy the corridors of American power.

. . . .

Originally, I had wanted to begin this second section of my work talking about how no one knows your kid better than you do, and momentarily I will indeed launch us in that direction as we discuss your kid, the lifetime's worth of data points you have on him/her, and how that relates to the brass tacks of handling money well. But this *Atlantic* article gave me pause. It reminded me that there are kinds of engagement between the generations that are healthy and sophisticated and generative, but, alas, there also are fusions that are mindless and toxic and domineering. One dividing line, if not the dividing line, has to do with respect (or lack thereof) by the older generation for the young person and her/his agency. For, ultimately, it is our kid's journey. It cannot be otherwise. Of course, this melding of generational agendas is complex stuff. It is possible that Thurston Howell III *authentically* wishes to carry the family torch in a manner remarkably similar to Dear Old Dad, aka Thurston Howell, Jr. Even so, in 21st-century America I think it fair to say that this will *not* be the rule.

I also thought this story of Anything-But-The-Open-Road-Journey might serve as a good reminder of who we are and who we are not. Self-recognition is psychological armor, and, in a time when media-blowhards sound their flatulent nihilistic horns on just about any meaningful or tender topic, I think it absolutely essential. But beyond simply fending off those who thrive on intimacy-shaming, I think we should go much, much further, to see that we are larger and better than we first thought, to borrow a phrase from the Old Bard. This is to say: We should feel tremendous confidence and goodness about the close relationships we have with our kids. And, although we ourselves live one or two valleys over from Perfection, our hearts and minds are fundamentally trustworthy. If we are blind or off-base, we cop to that. If we get enmeshed with our kid, and surely in moments that will occur, we tease that apart and make sure we're not expecting our kid to make life choices that mostly feed us. If on occasion we don't have a life, we get one. These small but very real personal acts transmit signals that encourage in our son or daughter the development of character and integrity. I sense that many of us already know this, but it seemed worth reiterating, if for no other reason than I believe this willingness to be both *guide* and *grasshopper* is what makes us truly larger and better than we first thought.

· · · · · · ·

To circle back on an earlier thread, I'm not a fan of the hands-off v. helicopter parenting dichotomy. Maybe I've too long lived in the American West where no one stresses if her kid decides to take a gap year between high school and college. Either way, I regard the hands-off v. helicopter polemic as a set up for a fight that need not be fought, especially since I don't think parental style is the pivotal issue. Rather, I think it's one of *attunement.* That, to my mind, is the key ingredient. Parents who tune into their kids in core, fundamental ways—who tune into who their kid may indeed be—have at their disposal the whole palate of wisdom and skillful means. Whether these parents draw more from 1950s handbook or 1960s style etc., it will be "right" because it will be accurate. That is, it will resonate with who a given young person is. If we are to censure a helicopter parent, it would be primarily due to the imposition of a values-driven agenda regardless of who that kid is or what he/she wants. In other words, that child's process of individuation would be irrelevant or deeply discounted by the powerful authority of such parents. This, you may recall, was a poignant, painful, and (for the 1950s era) normative theme running through the film,

Dead Poets Society. On the other hand, going "hands off" in and of itself is neither a solution nor an upgrade. I am not alone in having witnessed some highly problematic parenting (that looked an awful lot like non-parenting), justified in the name of "hands off" and "they'll figure it out." But again, I'm very uncomfortable with the whole polemic, as it quickly incites division and conflict, of which there is already more than enough in the world. So, for the purposes of this work, I posit *attunement* as the organic matter, the fertile element found in the ground of the parent-to-child relationship. If you wish to delve deeper into this matter, I refer you to the work of Harvard trained psychologist Daniel Goleman and his lot. They have written the first and second generation master works on emotional intelligence (EI), of which attunement is a core competency.

Not to deluge you with further homework assignments, but you might find it worthwhile to read the entire article by Ms. Flanagan in the *Atlantic* to see whether you agree with her contention that pushing a highly ambitious "success" plan on members of the younger generation (by their parents) fosters a culture of binge-drinking among them. How obvious is the line between transmitting core values to our kids that buoy, guide, educate and empower them *versus* laying a heavy trip on them? I'd like to think it's very obvious. That said, to a degree, we all carry conscious and semiconscious biases and values that doubtless color our dealings with our children. But this *Atlantic* story goes much farther than that. It gets political. It targets what it sees as a kind of family acculturation high on social and economic ambitions and low on character and moral spine. The disturbing part is that this swatch of American society seeks to lead. The critique by Caitlin Flanagan of this acculturation isn't pretty, nor, if you buy into her argument, should it be.

At this point I should like to do a quick dive into the subject of power itself. Certainly one of *the* central questions for any young person to contemplate in the depth of her being is: *How much capital/power do I seek in my life?* The question requires a bit of parsing. There are various kinds of power, just as there are various notions of success. To be part of a loving relationship is a kind of heart-vitalizing power, and a wonderful expression of success. To belong to a group or be a part of a close friendship or two is a kind of social and emotional power, and tremendously nourishing. To be your own person in this world, not deterred by the doubts of others, is a kind of inner-spirit power, one that I don't see enough of. To see through the instantaneous projections of others—unconscious psychic projections placed on you, some good and some not so good—is a kind of psychological power. *Yes, this is my stuff. I will think into it. No, that is your stuff. Not taking that on.* I could wax on, but, well, yes, I actually do need to stay focused and the focus is on capital power.

For, there's no denying the link today between money and certain kinds of overt social and political and environmental power. Money is a proxy for power in those domains. And, to be clear, I am not against power, just as I'm not against money (although our need to change the terms and spirit of money and capitalism, and to do so sooner, is whistling steam from the kettle on the cosmic front burner.) That we need X units of power and money to accomplish many endeavors, is fine. That the competition is fierce for said power and money, is also fine, and definitely a wake up call. Dilettantes on the capital side of life will be shredded by capital-centric devotees. Thus, the question gets refined to get us parents and guides thinking as well: How much capital power might a young bodhisattva be well served to acquire? I offer no universal answers, only the observation that each young person will ultimately have to decide for him or herself.

Whatever our young people decide, whether to live in a yurt in Nederland or a house with the white picket fence in Connecticut or a million possible scenarios in between, I wish to see them smart—really, canny as hell—in capital matters. Just because there are folks out there who live, breathe, and shit capitalism 1.0 (and have been bred to do this since the age of 13) doesn't mean our kids have to be tyrannized by that. But too many young people are vulnerable to funky outcomes, attributable to a variety of factors, perhaps the most conspicuous being: 1) self-sabotage, 2) misinformation, and 3) personal financial skill-sets missing. So let's not let that happen, or remedy it if it is happening. And that's what's up next. Time now to get into the brass tacks of our kids and personal money, of which the corresponding competencies are as follows: Saving & spending, planning & implementing, and investing & decision-making/judgment. We'll talk a little about making money and career and the kooky job market out there, but mostly as it relates to personal money. This is straight-up-the-middle Thoreau. As mentioned, he figured out he needed to work about 42 days of manual labor per year to cover his nut and have all the rest of his time to do "the real work" in his life. That kind of power, that kind of competence is what I have in mind here. And it begins with a fearless assessment of our kid's strengths, weaknesses, opportunities, and threats. No one knows our kid like we do! No one has data points like we do. No one has the bedside manner like we do. Then, over time, we figure out how to get them to do the periodic, fearless, self-assessment themselves. Without that, our kid has no motivation from within. Without that, he has no real need to take responsibility because he is answering to us; but at some point it's about him answering to himself regarding the earthy and essential question: *Just how good am I with handling my money?*

PART II

BRASS TACKS
OF PERSONAL FINANCE

 # Psyche + Money = Personal Finance

Up now is the "money thing." I'm going to go conventional in this section of the book and address the brass tacks of *saving, spending, planning, implementing, and so on*, because, in order to achieve and sustain economic autonomy, each young person must one day, preferably sooner, become proficient in the six areas of personal finance. However, I will not be delivering said content in a conventional manner. That would be ill-advised for several reasons. For starters, it's been done. At your local bookstore or on Amazon you'll find at least a dozen "bestseller" personal finance books. Some authors do a pretty solid job outlining the basics. Others get wonkish and their books read accordingly. Still other authors burst forth with their own stories of success. These narratives run the gamut from the self-effacing to the self-admiring. Whatever the angle taken, these books as a whole do seem to attract attention and I think it fair to say that the buyers of such books are genuinely trying to be saner with their money. This is good. This shows the sincere interest in what is an important topic.

But I have my reservations about the staying power of most

of these works, and here's why. They too often fail to factor in the impact of the powerful emotional drivers and deeply grooved cognitive styles that each of us *already* brings to our money world. It's as if doing money well were simply a matter of common sense. It's as if all economic agents were uniformly rational beings, ever thinking about maximizing utility. Nice tidy ideas, but not very useful. We humans have been known to do some pretty crazy stuff in the domain of personal money, and not for want of common sense or reason or IQ or book smarts! Indeed, we humans—yes, us as well as the kids—have been known to not only perform knuckleheaded maneuvers, but to unwittingly do repeat performances of said knuckleheaded maneuvers.

Matter of fact I did one just a couple of nights ago. On my screen was a set of summer concerts in New York's Madison Square Garden. The initial batch of tickets was offered to the public through a lottery, and I desperately wanted some tickets for these shows, so I went kind of crazy. In addition to my own lottery submission, I had my son, daughter-in-law, and my wife all put in for tickets. Seemed like a bang-up idea at the time. Covered all bases, or something like that. Later that night, however, as I lay in bed, I did the actual math of my actions. It wasn't pretty. If all my dreams came true, well, um, I could find myself the proud owner of about $3,000 of concert tickets. I broke into a sweat. $1,000 outlay for the tickets: Okay. $3,000: No, not remotely in the budget. Could I sell the tickets in the secondary market—i.e., Stub Hub? Sure, ultimately. But that would also mean: Say *hello* to my new, very un-fun, part-time job; one that'd cost me a fair bit of time doing emails and UPS letter-sends, and definitely cost me a little cash, seeing as I'd take a lower price to offload the tickets as quickly as possible. The next morning at breakfast I broke into a second sweat when my wife wanted to know if I had signed us up yet for a summer film seminar we were planning to attend. I said, *Hold off on that till all this concert tickets stuff settles.* My wife threw me a look. I assure you in her eyes in that moment I was no hero.

So let's start here, collecting *all* the historical data on our kid in the realm of personal money, and, if we care to do a parallel process, on ourselves as well. For I share my story with you not to emblazon a red "K" for Knucklehead on my chest for all the world to see, but rather to remind us that these financial matters can in moments be slippery, and we can fall, and, much as we'd like to forget the incident, we will do well to add it to the data set. On this last point I want to elaborate. Throughout this section of the book I'll be prompting you to think about how your kid has been doing, your kid's financial track record, and it is my sincere hope you will be fearlessly, even ruthlessly honest about it all. For, it would be natural to want to skew some of the data in the areas where our kid isn't doing so hot. We love our kid and want to think the best of him or her. But that would be a mistake. It's also wholly unnecessary, and here's why. No matter how our kid boots up in the house of personal money, the situation is workable. No one psychological style rules the money roost. There are various ways for our kid to arrive at a state of financial canniness. That is key, and worth repeating. There are several ways, actually at least four, to learn how to be super good at saving, spending, planning, implementing, and the like. But there is only one way, one particular mode of operating, that will best suit him/her. And that is the starting point: To recognize how our young person is "wired."

My experiences as a financial advisor and my observations as a family dude and person-in-the-world continue to support my view that there are four very distinct Types moving through the domain of personal money. I wrote about them extensively in my first psyche & money book, *Zen Money Blues*, and had fun with the project. The ZM Types also played a supporting role in my second book, *Lion Hearted Love*, a meditation on how money runs, for better and for worse, through married life. The fundamental premise of this Zen Money typology is that people bring a recognizable, fixed predisposition to the domain of personal money. It's there when you pay the bills or neglect them; correction, it's there *before* you pay the bills or neglect. It's the nature side of the financial equation, and, no, it's not a product of book smarts. The math of personal money management at this stage of life is easy: Spend less than you take in. But actually adhering to that? For some folks, no matter what they seem to do, they cannot escape living in the nettlesome gap between knowing and doing, otherwise known as not living within one's means. It is just this sort of phenomenon that we need to make a shrewd assessment of before we—as guides and parents—go into education mode. Which thoughts, words, deeds in our kid are changeable? Which are not? Where are the strengths to be identified and leveraged? As importantly, which aspects spell trouble and need serious upgrading if not containing?

A Word on Typology

Introvert or extravert. Thinking or feeling. Intuitive or sensing. Of course, this typology belongs to Carl Jung and proliferated in popular culture and the corporate HR departments by dint of the Myers Briggs test. My ambition in presenting my typology, aka the Zen Money Types, is naturally humbler. Above all, I want to get you and your kid looking at things in a fresh way. I want to challenge everyone to stop going into the same financial ditches. I want folks to know where the real levers of change exist, and don't exist. Changing the substratum of your self is probably impossible. But managing well what you've got, understanding what kind of operating system you've got—that looks like gold to me. And that's why I serve up the ZM Types. I'd like to get folks to thinking about what sort of "package" they've got. You know, I'm thinking about the programs that are constantly running in the background, processing what's going on, influencing what we see and how we see it and think about it.

There are discernments to be made. We'll vet the data, and do so by means of a Moderately Clever Parlor Game. As soon as possible, I want you to get hip as to which ZM Type your kid is. This will not only organize the data, but give us potent ideas about how we might educate our particular kid in matters of personal finance. Mastering the skills around spending, saving, and whatnot—learning in these areas is greatly enhanced when wedded to a keen understanding of the makeup of the person. Although missing in the conventional personal finance curriculum, in the conventional business world this is hardly an outrageous or novel approach. Case in point is SWOT. Frequently used by the legion of B-school trained consultants (who evidently love a good acronym like the next guy), SWOT means it's time to assess the business's Strengths, Weaknesses, Opportunities, and Threats. Likewise, I'm suggesting we pursue a loosely similar process of analysis based on our kid's financial track record. What are his identifiable strengths around money? How can we build on and speak to those strengths? Equally, what are the identifiable weak spots? How might we teach him to manage the weak spots in his mode of operating? The starting point is to see clearly what is, and what's possible. Don't worry. Every kid can achieve his/her financial ends. But the means will vary. That is why I offer up the Zen Money (ZM) Types. There are four in all, these ZM Types, and they give expression to recognizable, quintessentially human styles of relating to spending, saving, planning, and so on, in the personal money realm.

First, a light dive into the six competencies, during which I'll lay the ZM Types on you. Ready?

Here's the flashcard:

ZM Types	Natural Competencies
Creative	*Judgment*
Archer	*Planning, Implementing*
Architect	*Planning*
Maven	*Implementing, Saving*

. . . .

 Six Competencies of
Personal Finance
x Four ZM Types

I believe digging into the above *problem of multiplication* will pay nice dividends down the road for you and your kid. Although requiring a little sharpening of the pencil on your part, it is the superior approach, or so I contend. The reason is that the so-called common sense approach to money is too limited. It tends to overly concern itself with prescribing actions. *Early to bed, early to rise, makes a man healthy, wealthy, and wise.* Sure, okay, but what if you're not *that man or that woman?* That man might be an inveterate night person. Is he therefore doomed to ill health and bad finances? I don't think so. In contrast, there is the yogic approach to personal finance. It combines an awareness of the actions that need to be taken *with* an awareness of the agent, the doer of such actions. In other words, I want all of us thinking of the skills of personal finance in terms of what they mean for the *personalities* who do the personal finance. That's what was implied when, at the outset of this work, I used the phrase *subtle and practical arts* of money and personal finance. "Subtle" points to a keen awareness of who we are, of how we really tick—you could dub this our identity in the financial domain; "practical" refers to a familiarity with the tools and data sets of personal finance, and knowing how best to use them. This union of outer skills and inner awareness, aka this money yoga, opens up considerably more paths to "success" for the young people in the personal money realm.

As we explore these matters, I'll be nudging you to make discernments in the direction of answering the pivotal question: *Which Type is my kid?* Really, none of this is rocket science, but more akin to the aforementioned moderately clever parlor game. I think you'll get the hang of the ZM Types game pretty fast and in no time be able to narrow down your answer to two of the four Types. Nor does it stop there. With a tad more observation by you and additional color commentary by me, we'll bring the game to its natural completion as you sweetly and unerringly identify the ZM Type that fits your kid. Then we return to the overarching matter at hand, namely, educating the young people on the practical and subtle arts of money and personal finance. Now the pedagogy is straightforward. *Figure out our kid's ZM Type, understand what that means for him or her, and tailor the financial education accordingly.* Such a method is simple, direct, and quite potent.

Personal Finance

In order to achieve and sustain economic autonomy, our twenty-something (or early thirty-something) young person must ultimately become proficient in these six areas of personal finance:

> - saving
> - spending
> - planning
> - implementing
> - investing
> - decision-making

To be clear, proficiency does not automatically mean "proficient by one's lonesome." It might, but it's much more likely that excellent financial management will come about because you or I or our kid proceeds in a more extraverted and social way. *Hello, Beverly. You seem to have your financial house in order. Can you tell me: What are the merits of buying a condo vs. an apartment vs. a single dwelling home?* Some of these interactions will occur organically in the course of our day. Some of these interactions will be formal and we'll actively seek them out and pay for them. In all cases, extracting value from these interactions depends on us and our hard-earned stash of good judgment. But I want to circle back to something more basic about proficiency, a kind of lay-of-the-land truism: *Doing one's finances in isolation, and doing them well, is exceedingly difficult.* As it stands in the Zen Money universe, only one of the four ZM Types (the Archer) is poised to manage well her financial affairs for long stretches of time and do so in a solo manner. That said, she doesn't necessarily play it like that, even though she could. My notes from the field say that, especially with regards to medium and big financial decisions, Archers seldom go it alone, instead preferring to bounce things off their circle of trusted friends and advisors before taking action. I find that pretty dang interesting. Archers could manifest as the highly functional Do-It-Yourself, yet frequently take the team (aka social) approach. Anyway, in the ensuing chapters I will share a variety of snapshots showing how different "being proficient" can look. I'll also share some anecdotes illustrating how not to be proficient, one of which will include seeing my concert ticket buying spree through to its semi-hilarious conclusion.

· · · · · · · ·

Here now are some breezy notes apropos the six aspects of personal finance, and how some areas *naturally* suit some ZM Types though not others. Note: Do not sweat it if the Types and their corresponding qualities don't stick to your mind right away. The buzzword I hear bandied about in the world of arts and education these days is *immersion.* So, yes, please do immerse. I'll speak my weird Mark Butler language of personal finance and you, my friend, will simply let it wash over you as you float or sink or do a reverse double half pike twist off the high dive. *Capiche?*

SIX X FOUR

Saving. In concept it is easy to understand. Yet many a person has wondered: Why does the virtue of saving get embraced and acted upon by some people and not others? Cheat sheet: Archer and Maven ZM Types, by themselves, find it easy to see its power and convert that into a lifelong habit. Architects and Creatives, left to their own devices, do not. Still, the latter can be excellent savers, though they will require the help of others to pull this off.

Spending. The concept of spending smartly is basic, too. Here again we see that some folks absorb this multi-faceted skill set quickly and make it second nature, but some do not. Cheat sheet: Same as above, which is to say, Archers and Mavens incline quite naturally toward spending smartly. Over time they learn to transact shrewdly and spend within their means, while the Architect and Creative ZM Types *like to* spend but, no, they aren't "naturals" on the smart part. Again, for the latter two, the solutions are decidedly extraverted. Good financial friends slow them down, provide them with data points and strategies and rules of thumb, before actions are taken.

Planning. This aspect of personal finance takes a broader view of life and living, and integrates money into that picture. If saving and spending are the micro-behaviors of personal finance, then planning is the active, energizing vision that drives those behaviors in a certain direction. It is the fuel. It is the destination. It reflects its own particular feeling of Time. It is the implicit or explicit reason to save or to spend. If your mind is one constant machine for making plans, there's no missing that fact. If it doesn't really work that way, no worries. You still can be a highly effective planner in your life, albeit with the help of good planner friends. Cheat sheet: *Ladies and Gentlemen, your attention please. We have a material change.* The Archer and Architect ZM Types possess the stuff of planners. The Maven and Creative ZM Types do not.

Implementation. This should be regarded as the flip side of planning. Its purpose is to make any chosen plan a reality. Its activities are comprised of, but not limited to, the following: research, analyzing data points, paying the bills, making a budget and doing a budget, comparison shopping, full contact negotiation at time of purchase, knowing when something in the marketplace should be recognized as a service and when it should be treated as a commodity. There is a rigor involved here, and tremendous discipline. Superior implementers have both nature and a huge collection of market-based data points on their side. That potent mix ferments over time, producing their own nifty brand of *savoir faire.* Cheat sheet: Once more we have a material change. The Maven and Archer ZM Types naturally incline toward developing their implementation chops. The Architect and Creative ZM Types do not, and thus will have to very consciously journey (with their friends) to claim proficiency here.

Investing. During this period of one's Open Road journey, investing will likely have little to do with stocks, bonds, commodities, or rental properties. Rather, it pertains to the allocation of precious resources, whether they come from parents or one's savings or are borrowed from a financial institution. Go to college, or no? Take on debt, or no? Live at home, or no? Move to a big city to pursue a job or passion/gift, or no? Cheat sheet: In the decade of one's twenties, all Types are advised to talk these matters through with their thought-partners.

Decision-Making, aka Judgment. The items cited in Investing are the first big decisions to be made, and share a lot of common ground with the penultimate skill, that of superior decision-making or judgment. The idea here isn't just that our kids learn to allocate their resources wisely. It's that they learn to be great students of the game. They reflect on experience. They make mental notes about how the world functions, how friends and foes behave, and, as importantly, they develop keen insight into how they themselves function. Money is no different from any other domain of life: Each of us has our stellar and less than stellar qualities *before* we even enter the game. The trick isn't to somehow figure out how to grow to seven feet tall, so we can fulfill a childhood dream and play in the NBA. Instead, it's to come to terms with what we've got. Our strengths should be developed. Our weaknesses should be managed and our suspected blind spots exposed. The gift of wise decision-making is no gift at all; it is hard won via experience and contemplation. Cheat sheet: Same as above. All Types are advised to learn in and through relationships with Their People.

ZM TYPES	NATURAL COMPETENCIES
Creative	*Judgment*
Archer	*Planning, Implementing*
Architect	*Planning*
Maven	*Implementing, Saving*

. . . .

That's enough sorting by me of the characters (the ZM Types) and the issues (the necessary acquisition of the six competencies). Now it's time to develop hypotheses in the direction of answering the question on which quite a bit of our pedagogy depends: *Which Type is my kid?* Answer that and find, like the Yankee Clipper, the wind at your back. Answer that and we can assuage the fury of misunderstandings. But first I must ask:

Are you yourself feeling clever? Excellent. That's what I thought. Time then for a little parlor game.

Chapter 22 Is Your Kid an Over-Spender?

With that feisty little question, the parlor game of the Zen Money Types officially begins!

Either your kid already is "pretty good" at handling her money, or she is periodically out of control. Which one is your kid? You've dished out enough allowances, handed off car keys, and witnessed enough shopping excursions to weigh in on the matter. The evidence may not be definitive, but surely you've got loads of experiential data from which to draw a fair working hypothesis. Maybe at this point you are not keen on my bifurcation: *I don't know if my son, Little Johnny Appleseed, is an over-spender or not, because I don't know where all his money goes, but I do know he frequently runs out.* Fair enough. Mr. Appleseed, I think we are more or less getting at the same thing. Or to put it in the phrasing that I most commonly hear other parents use: *I don't worry about Miles. He doesn't come close to spending his allowance at college. But I do worry about Charlie. Always have.* It's the worry/don't-worry bifurcation. That, too, applies.

To reiterate, all of this is in terms of money. Seldom is this a comment on the young person's lovability, likeability, intelligence, or work ethic. So it is for Mr. & Mrs. Appleseed. They are very proud of Little Johnny. There's no denying he's a beloved character among his friends at university, generally respectful to adults, good in school, good in sports, and conscientious when he's got a part-time job. But his financial life? It's as if no one informed him that America is not a communist country and that the cash burning a hole in his pocket is private property; namely, his private property! Hold onto *his* cash? It doesn't seem to register. It is this lack of registering that later we'll make sense of. Meantime, Little Johnny freely parts with his cash, be it for concert tickets, food and bev, car to transport his merry band of friends, or gifts for his girlfriend. That is, until the seemingly inevitable day arrives yet again and his cash is gone.

By the way, if Little Johnny is your child, then worry is the accurate feeling—but up to a point. The good news is, there are remedies for Little Johnny; remedies not to change him into something he's not, but rather to help him mature, seriously mature; to help him take full ownership for who he is in this domain. I should know: Little Johnny and I are the same ZM Type (i.e., the Creative ZM Type), and my being a financial advisor by day, a profession that I love for a variety of social and intellectual reasons, does nothing to change the fact that I have to keep an eye on myself in the domain of my personal money. Self-management is the buzzword in the world of Emotional Intelligence (EI) and in leadership circles. Self-management very much applies here. Fortunately, the Creative has tremendous aptitude in these EI areas. This augurs well.

Architects Like to Fly

Quite apart from Little Johnny and me and other Creative ZM Types, there is another style that is overtly prone to over-spending or, its kissing cousin habit, simply not relating to money in an "ordinary," capital way. That is the Architect ZM Type. My daughter, Taia, is a member of this illustrious, sparkly tribe. In popular culture these are the quintessential spenders. Little Johnny was not a quintessential spender; his spending was semi-random, most often as boredom or the pulse of the moment dictated. For the Architect, and certainly for my daughter, something else is at play; namely, hatching plans. Loads of them. If you are this "planner" type person, you know what I'm talking about. My daughter, Taia, knows. She wakes up each day with a profusion of plans dancing in her head; plans that make sense; cohesive, comprehensive plans; plans for herself, her friends, her family, and on occasion the world. Did I say she's often very passionate about those plans? Yes, she looks pretty dang attached to making those plans a reality. I would be remiss to not plainly state that those plans take resources. Sometimes lots of resources. And, once upon a time, one Taia T. Butler flew over the fact that making those plans a reality took considerable resources; that is, until she financially crash-landed.

Now I'd like to believe she's done some learning and growing and thus is on the right side of things, but only time will tell. Her tendency to spend, however—or should I say the allure of her Planner Mind—is something I think she'll always need to be mindful of. Always. Even if she's making scads of money from the sweetest gig in christendom, she'll need to keep an unblinking eye on this. In a moment I'll lay Taia's college story on you. Beside its being a good illustration of one of the two spender/over-spender ZM Types, albeit in a late adolescent state of mind, I thought you might enjoy seeing me get my butt kicked. It is my acknowledgement that this journey is hard, with many twists and turns. Sometimes our labors bear fruit immediately, but sometimes we have to go to hell and back to enjoy the fruits of our labors.

Chapter 23 Saving, Spending,
& the ZM Types – Part 1

The rule in our house seemed reasonable enough. Cash gifts received by the kids for birthdays and holidays got allocated 50% to a savings account in their name and 50% to be spent on pretty much anything. In theory the kids could have saved 100% if they had wanted to, but I can't recall a time when this happened; which was fine by us, because our intended financial message to the kids was one of encouraging the middle way. *Save some of what you have for tomorrow, and enjoy some of what you have today.* Neither child challenged this approach. Perhaps it made sense to them. Perhaps it was simply a case of out of sight, out of mind. Perhaps they were pacified by the knowledge that at age 18 they'd have control of what indeed was their money. At any rate, I think it reasonable to wonder: When their moment of economic freedom came, and they left for college with 8k of savings each, just how well did our "middle way" practice in fact fare? You know, it's the proof in the pudding question.

Well, ours is really a tale of two children, but for now I will confine it to one.

The Plight and Heavenly Flight
of One Taia T. Butler

Sometimes the Young People really know how to push the envelope. Perhaps it's an envelope that back in the day we pushed with some vigor and evil delight, only now they do it even better than we did! God, I love family! Something about apples falling and trees. I thought that was supposed to be a good thing? Anyway, I'd like you to make the acquaintance of my very willful and wonderfully beguiling daughter, Taia. In the course of her young adult life, notably her college years, she has emerged as something of a spender. Boots from Steve Madden? Sure! Why settle for three pairs when you can get a fourth, and in teal! I exaggerate not! And for outfits, she has seemingly donned a fresh and sparkling and different one each time I see her. Hockey games? She loves the Colorado Avalanche. Do you know how expensive good seats are? My little princess surely isn't going to sit in the nosebleed seats. The list goes on.

Now, having just thrown her overboard, it's fair to ask: Is Taia a good kid? Yes, she's a good kid. Doing well in college? Yes, terrific grades and on the honors track and all that. Person of character? Yes, I believe she's an upright person, and willing to look at her less than stellar qualities. Good friend to her peers and all around decent human being? Looks like it. Vision for her life? In some areas, yes, she's mature—like what her professional/work interests are. I have no doubt she'll one day make a very nice living at whatever she pursues. But the spending thing ... Sam Holy Hill!

I suppose we should pause and turn the tables on Maria and me, and ask: In response to these spending activities, did Maria and I bring the right stuff?

Answer: Clearly not ... though not for want of trying!

Whenever a spending spree took place, we'd find out about it once the credit card bill arrived, and I was seriously annoyed. My go-to move was the proverbial Come to Jesus meeting. Usually you think of the Come to Jesus meeting as a one shot deal. In theory, no one should require multiple meetings with Jesus or those of us impersonating Jesus. Well, evidently Taia is a pretty powerful gal in her own right. Maria and I held multiple meetings of "reckoning" with her, and each one was as ineffective as the last. Sure, on her part there'd be periods of genuine self-reflection, remorse, and openness to change. But they'd be followed by sudden flights to shop for beautiful and expensive things.

That is, until Taia's savings ran out.

Accounting don't lie. In three short years' time Taia Butler ripped through her 8k. These were monies that we, her conscientious parents, had year in and year out helped her save from the parade of birthday and holiday gifts.

And now those monies were gone.

It was an especially impressive feat in that all her college expenses were already paid for. Okay, forgive the leakage of sarcasm. As a parent, I felt a little nutty, like my eyes were popping out of my head. Part of the madness I felt was an inability to convey what a future event—i.e., running out of your own money—would feel like and look like, much as I repeatedly tried. And I'm glad we repeatedly tried. But nothing got through like the unassailable fact that she'd run out of funds. So a big assist goes to the phenomenal world. It created the perfect conditions of economic tension (when we clearly could not!).

Seemed absolutely necessary.

Then we all could get a bit more real.

Actually, very real.

I regard this as the official start of Taia's education in the realm of money and finance. As to whether this is really the case, we shall see. But the funny thing is: I've already seen this cognitive-behavioral pattern in my wealth management practice. Some folks, no matter how old or smart or successful or rich, need us to play budget "games" with them, so they periodically can see and feel ground zero. They seem to like the finality of: *Hmmm, looks like I've run out of money this week. Or this month. Guess I'll stop spending.* It all makes me wonder if I should have played a preemptive version of such a game with Taia; you know, hid some of her own money from her? Just not sure. Didn't seem right to me. It was her money. All I could control were my actions, which in this case was a non-action: I wasn't going to rescue her from hitting ground zero.

 Saving, Spending,
& the ZM Types – Part 2

It was a bit bruising on the ego to be a family therapist by train-ing and a financial advisor in the prime of my career, and yet look up at the scoreboard to read: Your Daughter Is Kicking Your Butt. Beyond my bouts of self-pity and beyond the extra help-ings of humble pie, I have to say: We were lucky it was only 8k Taia Butler tore through! What if she'd had 30k of savings at her disposal? Or more? This is emblematic of the truly complicating world of *access to money* in relation to the young people. Every seasoned wealth manager has his or her story here. Parents have theirs. All riff off the theme of too much access to financial re-sources before someone's character is fully developed.

Does this mean Maria and I should have stashed in trust all those gifts for Taia? Or, as mentioned at the end of the last chap-ter, hid them from her? There's no short answer to that. But given the hand we were dealt, I think we did play it as best we could. We spoke our mind and otherwise refrained from cushioning Taia's fall to financial earth. Not long afterward, we informed Taia that her "planned" move to Denver post-college would not be funded solely by us. Matching funds? Perhaps. Taia then decided to move home for her last semester of college, to save us on room and board costs that we in turn put aside for her, assuming we liked her next plan. One imagines Taia felt the tautening effects of our response. One also imagines that at long last she was willing to relate to the earthy side of money. It did not hurt that at age 22 and counting, both life maturity and neurochemistry were increasingly and reliably on her side in a way that was not so at age 18, 19, or 20.

. . . .

As to the question that kicked off our little parlor game *(Is your kid an over-spender?),* if the answer is yes, or likely yes, then it's safe to narrow down your kid's ZM Type to either the Architect or the Creative. Now a few words on each ...

ARCHITECT ZM TYPE (AKA THE PLANNER TYPE, AKA THE CELESTIAL ARCHITECT)

In the domain of personal finance, the competencies of planning and implementing arch over the activities, say, of saving and spending. Indeed, they *contextualize* what is going on. Is Taia Butler a planner Type? Yes. Is she a spender? Also, yes. The point in mentioning both is that it is her *planner* style that drives what's going on. Spending is the expression of the fact that Taia is constantly making plans and constantly wanting those plans to become a reality. Try to fix her spending habits alone and you're simply pruning the leaves. It'll work for a while, but probably the thicket will grow back. Better, go to the root of the matter.

Lest I paint a two-dimensional picture of the Architect/

Planner, I should say that these folks plan in a number of directions, benefiting not just themselves but friends, family, spouse, children, and the world. This was and is true of Taia. She is the person in the family who, for example, makes birthdays rock. Whether it's getting the right cake or gift or calling up her brother to make sure he's in on a gift, she doesn't miss a beat. And the many gestures she makes (in this birthday example) convey the message that she has really exerted to think about me and what I might want/like/need. There is much generosity in this, both in spirit as well as—yup—spending. And that's one of the reasons to point out what's going on with this planner Type: She doesn't really think in terms of money. She thinks in terms of plans, and making them real.

To summarize: The Architect ZM Type likes to plan. Her mind naturally works this way, and the plans she produces are often beautifully detailed, as well as comprehensive in nature. There is also the matter of volume. That is, she has been known to make lots of plans. And that is where the trouble, in part, lies for this Type. Having a number of plans in her mind, she feels quite passionate about all of them. Willful is another word that comes to mind. And while I'm talking about the emotions, I think it also fair to say that shopping provides her with a way to cheer herself up. For, it's something she's good at and something that usually makes her feel good. Of course, the shadow side of this looms. Consumerism promises much, but what it delivers is mixed and often disappointing. Taken too far, it throws one financially out of control. Not only does it get expensive, it potentially imperils one's chances for fully implementing one's most cherished plans. I also suspect that the buoying effects of "retail therapy" too often just don't last that long. This is a conundrum worth noting, especially since the Open Road journey is chock full of dark nights and anxious days. Against that backdrop the Architect ZM Type is thus prone to overspend; you know, it's her less than sophisticated but very understandable coping mechanism.

To come, we'll explore how to work with the wonderful and passionate and willful energy of the Architect/Planner Type. Now let's take a gander at the other Type who, left unchecked, left to his own devices, is prone to overspending, or, as the case may be for him, to running out of money. *Voilà*, the Creative ZM Type.

CREATIVE ZM TYPE

I am the Creative ZM Type. So is my godson Spencer, and Little Johnny Appleseed. And as to how we can wreak financial havoc on ourselves and distress the heck out of our parents—we do this qualitatively differently than the Architect Type. Our trouble spots are not imbedded in our strengths, like they are for the Architect, because we're not known to shine brightly when it comes to planning activities. No doubt, it can be energizing at times, and we might even be good at planning the occasional trip or fun outing, but, no, in a broad and overarching way, it's not a prime motivational force in our life. The Creative Type doesn't get all jazzed by making scads of plans the way the Architect Type does.

So if the Creative isn't driven by a passion for planning, then what gets him into spending trouble? For starters, he doesn't naturally tune into money. You might think that's also the case for the Architect when she shops, but actually the not-yet-mature Architect *tunes money out* when she shops. Just ask Architects and they'll often report that they have little to no recollection of looking at price tags, or registering mentally what things cost. That tuning out makes her experience all the more enjoyable, in that her shopping experience becomes frictionless—in fact, there is no pain, no tug as she parts with her money, because she doesn't feel her money leaving her! But the Creative works differently. He just doesn't see money as that real. On the one hand, this lets him see the World of Possibility, and in my day job as a financial advisor this lets me periodically relax all the "rules" of personal finance and money management so that my clients and I can think freshly about the matters before us. I find the well-timed *dropping of the financial superego* quite invaluable in the professional setting.

But when this mode of perception is used habitually, or done without an awareness of what one is up to—then, no, this way of looking (or not looking) at capital is dangerously one-sided. Missing is a proper understanding of money's relative usefulness in a good human society. Missing, too, is the recognition that the Creative lives in a time and place when acquiring good money management skills is an indisputable necessity for making it on the Open Road of life. Little Johnny Appleseed, as discussed earlier, is a good kid; but he's yet to come to terms with the truth of his environment. His mentality has been and still is that of a hunter/gatherer. Indeed, Little Johnny would like to follow the migration of the buffalo from south to north and across the great plains. This is how he would like to make his way on the Open Road journey, metaphorically speaking. And it is a beautiful metaphor, with echoes of the great Native People of the American West mixed in with the wandering, joyful spirits of Whitman and Kerouac and their avatars; except taken too far, it reveals a serious schism. I don't think I need to point out to you the full incongruence of this mode in 21st-century America. On the other hand, I also don't think I need to point out that, now more than ever, we don't want to lose the light of luminaries like Spencer or Little Johnny Appleseed, either.

To summarize: Quite apart from the Architect who has plans for her life, her kids, holidays, outfits, experiences, what have you, the Creative is no planner and feels no pressure to make a plan a reality. Rather, he exhibits a very strong tendency to spend freely and spontaneously. He's also moved by a wonderfully irrational side; he may help his daughter financially make it through medical school even though he could use those funds for his own adventures, but he feels it's important to keep his daughter from being saddled with debt. And even though he didn't plan for that moment, he doesn't care: He's going to help anyway. And if that means he lives more simply at retirement, or works an extra five years, that's okay, too. So the Creative does have virtues, some of which are big hearted, though he can be a Spender Without a Cause, whereas the Architect ZM Type is a Spender With a Cause, because her plans most definitely are her causes.

. . . .

Since I'm at it, here are some quick notes on the other two Types—the Types that are *not* in danger of over-spending or running out of money.

ARCHER ZM TYPE

Taia's brother, Mikyo, is an Archer (the only one in my immediate family, as it happens). This does not make him morally superior to the rest of us, even though we all are envious! Being the Archer means that, a) he does indeed possess the natural planner chops in that he consistently and excellently plans, and, b) he also comes through as a superb implementer. Implementer here is code for a particular kind of saving and spending. We could call it full bodied, or rigorous. For, Mikyo is willing to part with his cash to make his plan a reality, but first he does his homework on quality and price. Case in point: When he bought his first new car he researched wide and then deep, settling on the Volkswagen GTI with the 2.0 liter engine made in Wolfsburg, Germany. Now I don't mean to sound like a car magazine, but several trusty sources on the internet agreed that the Wolfsburg factories were deserving of their reputation for superior craftsmanship, to wit, that the heavy frame of their GTI, the smart torque, and robust horsepower were all pleasingly in balance. For a fair price Mikyo thus ended up with a sweet car.

I won't tell you my car-buying horror shows, but will only add that I've learned my lesson and these days I simply tell Mikyo how much I'm willing to spend and he points me in the direction of two or three cars to consider. Even then, I'm a completely worthless negotiator on price, so I stand down while my wife, Maria, charmingly tackles the car salesman. But here's the best part. The outcome is usually awesome. Working with others works well for me. I engage whatever the issue is, i.e., spending decisions or bigger strategic life decisions, but I focus on the process. That is my discipline of mindfulness and awareness. Money matters, for me, are best done as a social experience. I proceed that way whenever possible. But I digress.

Regarding the Archer and his/her innate planning abilities, I'm struck by how cool-headed he can be in comparison to the Architect/Planner Type. The Archer is the kind of person who can walk away from a deal if it doesn't, in his estimation, add up. He can be brilliantly dispassionate. The Architect/Planner, at least when dealing on her own, has an extremely difficult time doing that. She wants what she wants, kind of like now.

Along with the Archer, the Maven ZM Type is your natural saver. Motivations for this behavior differ, however. Some Maven folks love to save. Others, like my wife, simply hate to spend! But what all Maven/Implementers have in common is a penchant for driving a hard bargain, a knack for finding a great deal, *and* they do this consistently and excellently.

Mavens count everything that goes in and out, or at least they are inclined to. Money for them is decidedly "real." Therefore, if a couple works together on some or all of their finances, the Maven is the natural "manager" of the purse. Note #1: I did not say boss of the purse. That would take things too far. But the Maven is the one who is inclined to have a budget and know where things stand financially. If she doesn't, then she should, ASAP. Note #2: There can be a bit of personal confusion that arises for the Maven/Implementer. That is, she's prone to think that saving money is the same thing as having a plan. Same can be said for spending smartly. That is a wonderfully useful talent, but, no, that isn't a plan either.

By contrast, innate planners (Architects and Archers) have designs. If they save, they save for a specific reason: Old Man Appleseed knows that Little Johnny Appleseed will one day grow tall and go to college, and that will cost a pretty penny; or, there should be funds for a rainy day/opportunity fund; or, there will be experiences/travel/service work he will want to do in a later chapter of his life, and so on. This is not to say that Mavens don't have goals. Of course they have goals. I am reminded of a young woman who left home at seventeen and has been saving for 10 years for the down payment on a home. That is a very real goal, but arguably in her pursuit of this goal, she sold herself short by avoiding the costs of trade school and thus kept herself stuck in a service job that offers little career or financial upside. On several occasions I've attempted to point this out to her, but to no avail. To her, the goal is the plan. But it's not. There's no vision. I think her lack of investment in her career/trade speaks quite directly and painfully to this.

. . . .

I hope this palette of qualities in the saving and spending universe will help you to get a feel for the strengths and weakness of the ZM Types, and where your kid might land. To come are further descriptions, along with some how-to offerings for relating to your young person in the midst of these dynamic conversations. How do we talk to them, anyway?

Chapter 25 Outline & Pith & Education

You've doubtless got a line on whether or not your kid is an over-spender. Let me load you up with more provisions; i.e., additional cognitive/emotional/behavioral descriptors, keywords, modes of perceiving and functioning, brilliance, blind spots, preferred language and logical flow for each of the 4 ZM Types. I know that sounds like a lot, but I'm going to keep it on the lighter side. Your job is to do the immersion thing I talked about. Just let it wash over you. Let it refresh you like cool sheets of mist and spray kicking up from sea. After all, we've boarded the Yankee Clipper one last time and in a trice I'll sail us through some cool coastal waters, getting us to look back at the shore and adding some final ZM Type thoughts on how we might best advance the dialogue with our kid.

Here now the mist and spray:

ARCHITECT TYPE

In the domain of personal money she's a heart & mind person, he's a heart & mind person. This twin-engine drives the Architect's management of her/his personal financial world. The question is: Will her natural planner-strengths help or hinder as she moves through her life, money included? If this is your kid, plan on tackling her early and often. Yes, tackle. Call meetings. Get the numbers down on paper. Yes, that's called a budget. B-u-d-g-e-t. The Dalai Lama has one. You should too. Indeed, the Architect ZM Type knows that she should have one and live within the constraints of said budget, but will she cut through the thousand reasons (aka awesome plans) that push back and get her to flirt with going out of bounds? Probably not, unless you show her how it's done, unless you then hand her the razor sharp knife and tell her to start cutting through her elaborate stories. Another example? How about April in Paris? Okay, that's a Thelonious Monk reference; I got confused. How about April and that means tax time? Time to tackle. Grab your mobile device. Let's find out if she filed her taxes on time. Go further. If she filed for an extension (because it seemed like a good idea at the time, and perhaps it was), then find out if she did the full calculation that tells her if she should have included a check for more taxes with that extension. Assume nothing. Make sure she wasn't a 1099 employee or failed to take deductions from her paycheck (because, again, it seemed like a good idea at the time).

I know, I'm being quite energetic, and you'll have to decide what suits you and your kid. But the warrior energy is rising in me, pushing me to encourage you to be active and energetic too, because I hear the clock ticking and that points to a well-researched and documented reality: The neuroplasticity of our kid's brain can still be refreshed and reformed and rewired (without injuring her spirit) all the way till around age 35.[6] Thus, I recommend you plan on fighting the good fight. Challenge your kid to counterbalance her passion (in the moment) by deploying

---

6 Again, wheeling off of Dr. Daniel Siegal's vast body of research on the brain, along with Dr. Meg Jay's clinical work and aggregated research.·

her intellect or adopting rules, protocols, etc. (in advance). For, the activity of planning itself frequently generates *passion* and that passion in turn has been known to give birth to a welter of intense emotions that say *I want* and *I must have.*

Passion, love, longing, care—these are beautiful and potent emotions, though one can easily get drunk on them. Therefore, do require her to discover in herself that reservoir of cool intellect. Challenge your kid to look at the numbers, the credit card bills, what she actually spent. Further: Lay said statements out on the kitchen table for review if you can. Did she stay in budget? Did she have thoughts about budget while shopping? Did she even have a budget to begin with? Or, to pivot toward the matter of implementation: Did she needlessly pay full retail? The point is: Analyze, analyze, analyze. I know, it sounds dreadfully boring. Maybe it is. Even so, we do this because we hope one day soon she will adopt the habit (don't laugh) of analyzing, and will regard it as a friend to bring on the journey.

The Architect is far and away the most willful of the 4 ZM Types. So, I say: Challenge her now while your inputs can indeed leave meaningful imprints—imprints that over time our kid will respect, reflect on, and perhaps even make her own. It's going to be a long game—her education. That's not a problem, but do plan on that. Here, now, is a short narrative on our dear Architect's financial competencies:

Saving – Could actually be a terrific saver, but it must be connected to a plan. Her plan.

Spending – The most willful spender of all the ZM Types. She sporadically (or never) tracks the numbers and prices involved in spending behaviors. Frictionless shopping is Enemy #1.

Planning – This is where she will make it or break it on the journey. Will she be the mature planner who prioritizes and assigns varying time intervals to plans, *or* will she cling to the subtle but hindering vestiges of childhood, in essence demanding that she wants to have it all and have it all now, also known as: I just want the the fairy tale. (Note: wanting the fairy tale is equal opportunity; the dude population of Architects wish for the fairy tale just as frequently as the dudettes.)

Implementing – This is not her strong suit. She'll likely pay retail without a fuss. But that doesn't let her off the hook. When it comes to purchasing bigger ticket items, she will do best to muster her people. In particular, she will benefit greatly from good Maven and Archer ZM Type friends who shower her with encouragement, advice, connections, and market information. On the very gritty kitchen sink level of her life, it will take a concerted effort to cultivate and maintain good financial hygiene; i.e., pay the bills on time, register the car on time, file her tax returns in a timely manner, etc.. I have also observed that the last 5% of a financially-related task can be the bane of her existence.

Investing & Decision-making – In our kid's twenty-something time of life, these two aspects repeatedly intersect and raise the question: Has our Architect kid made the decision to seriously learn and grow in regards to the capital side of life? If he/she has decided yes and thus made the serious commitment such that it permeates her actions, then that's all you can ask. The Good Judgment borne of experience & reflection will assuredly then come with time, step by step, piece by piece.

MAVEN TYPE

The Maven ZM Type frequently appears as the kid we *don't* worry about. For him/her and perhaps for us, there is some confusion about how competent he is, because he's naturally thrifty. That fact can send us in the wrong direction. Not being a screw up, he himself might semi-reasonably arrive at an inflated sense of how good he is with money. True enough, this is the kid who will probably not make the big mistakes, but over 5- and 10-year arcs of time, he may be subject to the long fall to financial (and life ... yes, life) mediocrity. His lack of natural planning chops, and his lack of awareness about this fact, leave him vulnerable to making skewed life decisions. On occasion his seeming strength turns against him. His demand for having and saving money can imprison him, or narrow his horizons. Money—as in having it and saving it—can become something of a fetish for him. Same goes for negotiating the heck out of every deal with every person he comes into contact with, including boyfriends/girlfriends, parents, and friends. I'm being a little dramatic but you get the point: Money and control are super important to the Maven ZM Type, and those factors can become seriously constraining for him and for those who enter his world.

However, once the Maven ZM Type learns that indeed there is more for him to learn, and then, building on that moment of enlightenment, he decides to become the sincere (though still quite precocious) student of the financial game, he'll learn, 1) to relax his desire for control, at least in moments, and 2) to allow Trusted Others in his world to round out his view of life and money and what's ahead. In terms of educating and engaging the Maven ZM Type, I think he benefits most from gentle, spacious, and warm encouragement. The warrior energy that I summoned when talking about the Architect ZM Type has little place here.

Playfulness and gentleness and a sweet dose of cunning are more to the Maven's liking. Integrating the emotions (i.e., passion for experience) is a good idea, though beware that it could backfire. For the Maven sees getting-such-a-deal as one of the great adventures out there. I'm reminded of a friend's son who attended Princeton. Clearly a smart kid, he nonetheless couldn't help himself when it came to getting the new iPhone at a fantastic price, which meant driving across New Jersey in the pelting rain because he knew just where to go. Now was this an optimal life/financial behavior? Probably not. His studies at uber-expensive school took clear precedent, but they got ditched for a few hours as he sought the Holy Grail of iPhone Deals. His parents got a nice dose of stress for the afternoon, worrying about their star kid buzzing around on the Garden State Parkway. They'd begged him not to do it. For naught. He couldn't not do it! True, none of this was the end of the world, but there can be quite the negative compounding effect by such behaviors over time.

Overt money matters are clearly an area of interest, and thus we, in our role as parent guide and banker, can teach through that medium. Co-underwriting projects, big purchases, and adventures can be just the ticket for a Maven to be expansive when he would otherwise hold back. To be clear, I'm not saying that we alone should pay for the Maven's raucous time at Burning Man or buy him the new BMW. He likes freebies like the rest of us, so that won't teach him much. But in ventures where he puts a little skin in the game and where we put a little skin in the game, there will likely be openings for us to gently weave planner elements into the conversation. In moments he might relax the financial controller that he ever has working, and perhaps even explore aspects of his usually suppressed vision or passions.

Saving – When in doubt, when in certainty, he saves. He likes having money in the bank. He likes seeing the cash in his wallet. If a debit card or e-cash user, he knows exactly what's in his account.

Spending – He is the original tough customer. Due diligence is his middle name. He can also have some pretty crazy spending rituals in pursuit of The Best Deal.

Planning – He is not easily disabused of the notion that saving and planning are *not* the same thing. But indeed they are not. Saving money is not itself a plan. Rather, savings should be regarded as resources for a future idea, opportunity, or plan. The Maven ZM Type might not buy that. Too often, and detrimentally so, he'll let financial considerations govern the life decisions/actions instead of wading into complexity. That's a shame, and quite unnecessary. With a little help from his friends, the Maven can learn to slow down and thoughtfully interweave many life elements (of which money is but one) when making an important decision. In Part One I mentioned a young woman I know—a very talented young woman—who left home at age 17 to fend for herself, and each step of the way figured things out and did very well in her career. But one day, ten years down the road, she hit the career wall because she lacked some of the skill sets (i.e., writing proficiency; being handy with stats) and social connections (yes, strong ties and weak ties) most often picked up in college. Her desire to save, in her case for a down-payment on a home, precluded anything else, even investing in herself for the long run. I think she most definitely short-changed herself.

Implementing – Straight up, the Maven is the best at getting things done on the financial front. Once he learns a given task, he takes control. He's a genuine captain. To name a few tasks in his wheelhouse: He pays the bills on time, tracks the budget like Sergeant Major, and he knows where to shop, when to go quality and when to buy knockoffs, and what you should pay for an astounding array of exotic and ordinary items, i.e., phones and phone plans; airfare: how and when to fly to ___________ for a good price and minimal hassle; where to live—buy or rent; which clothing labels are crap and which are legit; where to stay in the big city, from hostels to couches; cars: just buy whatever car he buys, perhaps even get him to buy the car for you (I feel sorry for the sales guy already); and more.

Investing & Decision-making – Usually the Maven ZM Type plays it one of two ways. Either he is keen on having a boatload of money, or, he's keen on not spending any more than he has to so he doesn't have to make any more money than need be. Yes, he's a serious controller. And that is fine so long as he understands that, left to his own natural devices, he is not nor will he be the Chief Financial Officer of his world. Why? Because the CFO (of a real live company) is the one who thinks in terms of vision and strategy as well as execution and accountability. The Maven naturally possesses the latter but not the former. In order to develop a sense of vision and strategy (i.e., do good planning), the Maven will need to enlist the help of others. That in and of itself will be a challenge for him. Last word on the Maven, and it relates to his shadow side. Oscar Wilde once defined a cynic as one who knows the price of everything and the value of nothing. That in a nutshell is what the Maven ZM Type must learn to transcend. And he can—with the help of his friends. If he lets them help him.

ARCHER TYPE

First things first: Just because The Archer possesses the complete package doesn't mean she already knows it. Sometimes Archers have no clue about the person in the mirror. In my second work, *Lion Hearted Love,* I recounted how for the first half of my childhood my mother was by all accounts the *untested* when it came to financial matters. The stern cultural norms and skewed gender role prescriptions had left women like my mother out of the financial game. The result was that no one had any idea that my mother (and Archerly women like her) had serious game. As fate would have it, we'd all learn just what she had after my father's untimely death. Which brings me to my point: Make sure your kid gets tested with regards to handling real-world financial matters, and this should begin with the college or post-high school years. I'd really like to say it should start with the first car and your express commitment to pay for some or all of college, but that could take us in a whole other direction that I just can't give justice to now. Anyway, please, don't do it all for your kid. In the next chapter I'm going to return to a kindred theme discussed in Part One—namely, economic tension—and this idea of letting our kid get tested by situations conveys a similar sensibility. Let your kid try her hand at things. See what kind of game she's got. Count on her making mistakes. What will she learn from them? Will she make the same mistakes twice? If truly an Archer, probably not. Count also on her gaining increasing levels of proficiency as per saving, spending, etc. What will she learn from her successes? You get the drift.

Should your young person prove to be the Archer ZM Type, then you've got some serious education sessions—as in rangy and at times deep discussions—ahead of you. Yes, this is one of those super good problems, discussing life and money with a person—

your kid!—who brings to the feast a pleasing mix of warm emotionality and sharp intellect. Her education will generally be low drama. As noted previously, the awake Archer seldom gets caught in the passion-extremes of the planner/Architect, nor in the controller-extremes of the implementer/Maven. Her education will thus be rather straightforward. She can certainly learn to plan and plan cogently and powerfully and beautifully, and she can turn on the Maven intensity at the time of implementation when she has her facts straight and she wants to turn on that intensity. So, do enjoy the straightforwardness of educating her; and, if you run into the limits of your own knowledge about a particular area, and you undoubtedly will, then don't worry about it, just acknowledge it and figure out who knows what about the matter at hand. That is, think of the people in your own financial world and call on them, whether friends, family, or professionals. Yes, I'm pounding the table one last time in support of the social approach.

For the Archer who puts in the time to learn the ins and outs of her financial craft, the rewards will indeed make her look like the poster child for personal finance. However, she or he will remain fully human and achieve no godlike status in this domain. Neither will her Maven, Creative, and Architect kin get put in some sort of inferior box. This isn't how it works. The Types aren't meant as yet one more way to inflict pain on oneself or others. Rather: Each Type has its brilliance and strengths as well as vulnerabilities and blind spots. This is a very human complexity that warrants patience and understanding and integrating. The Archer, as she herself learns and grows and gets her ducks powerfully in a row, might also grow impatient with the "messiness" of others. Archers who are on their game can wonder what the heck is wrong with the rest of humanity. Because all things financial come somewhat easily for them, and because they know how to make the financial whole greater than the sum of its parts (not a small feat), they can't understand why others, including friends/family/partners, struggle and muddle as they do. They can't understand how others can be repeat offenders. Now I'm not saying it's easy to suffer fools, but such a notion really doesn't apply here because the other Types are not fated to some disastrous end. They're not. But, as discussed, they do have to move through their respective financial worlds in a social and circuitous manner. Then they can achieve the level of financial sanity and competence and, yes, success on par with any other ZM Type.

So we've gone FROM the possibility of the Archer being a babe in the financial woods, not knowing that she possesses superhero-like powers until she comes into her own and activates said powers, TO her being a smidge arrogant in relation to friends, family, and people she otherwise loves. Whether this negative shadow is benign or becomes malignant depends on a host of factors, many of which have little to do with money. But where it's harsh, it's ugly to behold. I can think of several men from my father's generation who can communicate nothing but disdain for their adult kids who continue to muddle and struggle, as if financially struggling is a character flaw (which is what the Archer can unwittingly conclude). Thus, in our conversations with the Archer-in-training, we want to round and soften her view of herself and others. The world concerns both money and non-money. Life concerns many things, of which money is but one. More: The Archer ZM Type has a good bullshit-o-meter. Even as she learns her way, she loathes the idea of fostering financial dependence in others and otherwise rewarding profligacy. That's fine. But then she will benefit greatly from understanding where to be accommodative of her significant other, new spouse, best friend, or sibling, versus where to be sharp and cut and lay down the law. No surprise, I think teaching her a light version of the ZM Types might do wonders. For, sooner or later, she's got a lot to give others. She's the perfect teacher in all things personal money. But she won't be terribly effective if she simply thinks others are screw-ups. That sort of black and white thinking will come back to hurt her, if for no other reason that we humans do tend to irrationally and intensely love others and some of those beloved others won't be Archers.

Saving – She/he has got an appreciation for saving, with a natural propensity to plug that into the bigger picture (i.e., goals, plans, opportunities, rainy day); easily prompted by her/his people.

Spending – She spends smartly because she possesses the outrageous willingness to walk away from the deal, adventure, or plan if it doesn't line up with bigger picture (i.e., the plan/purpose of the expenditure); her spending activities are not only guided by price, but purpose too.

Planning – She kicks butt in the planning department because she's not battling the Architect's demons of extreme attachment; her plans are grounded in reality, though she'll certainly have her occasional extravagance.

Implementing – She knows budget-tracking, bill-paying, etc., are her tools, and she doesn't mind getting to it! In fact, those tools further enhance her ability to make solid decisions. She's also pretty handy when it comes to price and knowing when to pay retail and when to wait for the deal. True, she doesn't live for this side of the life the way the Maven ZM Type does, but she's awfully effective when she wants to be.

Investing – Be it putting money away for a sunny day or rainy day, or spending on additional education or training, the investment ideas hook in with the Archer's bigger picture; she's into strategy and immediately grasps that Time must be factored into all risk/ reward equations.

Decision-making – When she embraces the strengths and possibilities of her Archer-ness, she usually accepts the responsibility that comes with having great natural talents. This is good. If she hesitates, then confront that hesitation. Are there antiquated self-concepts holding her back? Is she feeling ambivalent about selling her soul for the payoffs of the capital world? Does she simply not want to shoulder the burden of her financial life just yet? Whatever it is that keeps her pausing at the threshold, do discuss. Beyond that, she just needs to become her destiny, which includes being a rock steady decision-maker. This is where her crown jewel lies. Good judgment can be hers, so long as she doesn't fall prey to arrogance and defining too much of life in terms of money.

CREATIVE TYPE

This is the Type who—once really awake—most resembles the Archer … though he is not, nor ever will be, the Archer. Why? Because the mature Creative works it: He *exerts*, time and time again. Exerts how? Exerts to move to the neo-cortex/frontal lobe of his brain, aka, to do the necessary "slow thinking." Slowing it all down = good luck and good fortune.

Up till now I've given each Type a fairly rangy description, but in the case of the Creative ZM Type there really isn't all that much surface area to cover in regards to his education. The nub is this: *He must come to terms with the truth that he should never freewheel in isolation.* That's called courting financial disaster. Or ending up back in his parents' house and encamping in the room he grew up in. Or getting ditched by his girlfriend for not having his financial shit together. Or getting a bailout from the Bank of Mom & Dad for some nasty credit card debt that he was on the wrong side of and was compounding at a rate of 24% per annum (that cost him his dignity for a time and for a spell his folks were not appreciating him and his dang financial incompetence). Or ending up sleeping in his dad's woodworking shop. Or getting so excited that he might have ended up with $3,000 of concert tickets.

Creatives, when asleep and feeling bold, are a Greek tragedy waiting to happen. They can write the book (!) on suffering because there are few mistakes they haven't made. But they are a resilient lot once they have their awakening. That's the crux of the matter. Everything in the Creative's financial world calls for him to slow down and talk to the people he trusts and slow down some more and only then move into action mode. I know, sometimes the decision is small and immediate: *Yo, you in line, you gonna order a sandwich or not? Come on, spit it out. Don't mumble. You want mayo, tomato, lettuce and what?* Sure, in those situations the Creative will do well to have his weekly allowance for "schtuffs when out and about" and that includes roast beef sandwiches and coffee/tea and the like, and when that cash is gone, he can act like a penniless character in a Steinbeck novel, which he's perfectly fine with, too. And that leads to an important point: Although we Creatives do know how to suffer, and suffer by our own making, that doesn't mean that we have the obvious pain points. Creatives are generally okay with being out of money—unless being out of money means in the big big big sense being out of money. Then the Creative is going to shriek like the next guy. But as far as day-to-day stuff, and not being able to go to the concert or bar because he's out of cash, no, that may not be a motivating factor (i.e., pain point) for him to wake up.

Yes, indeed, you will talk with him about saving, spending, planning, implementing, investing, and decision-making, and that will be good and probably very helpful; but again the real focus is on process, on slowing him down, on reminding him to focus on process and thinking about whom he can talk to and about what. Process is the vehicle that takes him to financial sanity and in his own way becoming rock steady. Process is code for others, for mustering friends and counselors. Process is code for slow thinking, for consciously moving as much mental activity as possible to the frontal lobe. This should be a lifelong practice. With the Creative, it's strangely black and white. If he gets this, Bob's your uncle. If he doesn't, it won't be pretty.

Saving – Thinks about saving when prompted (by his trusted people), but not a moment before!

Spending – Can be an over-spender as well as an under-spender, depending on the whim of the moment (and when not employing his thought-partners); doesn't solidify spending, or demand high-cost experiences, but values the richness of life (which often has a price tag); cash burns a hole in the Creative's pocket.

Planning – Enjoys making plans (ever heard of the Creative Engine?), though is able to let them go if prompted to think in terms of the bigger picture or other pictures; can shift and change more easily than the Architect in this area.

Implementing – Might throw bills into a paper bag and forget about them, or miss tax deadlines if not prompted; he generally benefits from structure and support from others; awake Creative is open to guidance and can be a decent workhorse in these matters; just needs a program to follow, a routine to stick to.

Investing & Decision-making – Inherently possesses good *life* judgment because of his/her strength in the Emotional & Social Intelligence arenas; however, the manual labor for him is to integrate money and finances into the realm of good life judgment; the Creative can get the most out of his people, but he has to activate them as situations unfold.

Chapter 26 Switch Gears

The wine's all gone, the tea is cold, the treats are stale and the stories and the jokes are no longer funny as they once were. At this point in the game (or the party) my father-in-law, Svend, ever the consummate host, might bring out a nip of aquavit to revive the crew, while my mother-in-law, Debby, working at cross purposes to him, would serve said drinks on cocktail napkins that read in a loud, cheery font: *Time To Go Home!* Anyway, I guess it's time to bring our ZM Types parlor game to a close and for everyone to head on home, but not without my first saying I hope the game was useful and to let you know there is a party prize (ahem) waiting in the back of this book. It is a humble party prize, comprised of some final sketches on the ZM Types and how we might engage and encourage our young person on the path to financial competence, if not mastery. You know, to help them become canny as hell in financial matters, so they can be free—as Henry Thoreau asserted—to do the real work.

Let's now switch gears. The topic was discussed in Part One and it feels important that it make an appearance once more. Why? Because money matters provoke the emotions, and the emotions can be negative and, if mismanaged, can work against us. Take fear. It's an exceptionally fierce emotion, with countless ways of moving through us and moving through our kid. The overarching journey to individuation and independence is quite demanding, and as we'll be reminded a couple of chapters thence, it's not easy to take flight and stay in flight, much less hit cruising altitude. This whole road to independence, particularly with authenticity and spirit and a whole mix of life and planetary considerations mixed in, isn't just demanding: It takes time. Time and attention. So we'll go there, but on our way let's first visit the hall of mirrors. Fear has a way of transporting us to our very own hall of mirrors, where we see our kid and we see ourselves and it's sometimes hard to know precisely what's going on. Even so, let's go there. Why? Because embracing fear is a part of the journey. In terms of money and capital, I think the fear-edge comes out in regards to the following dynamic interplay encapsulated in the question below.

· · · · · · ·

How do we as parents/guides "create" the right kind of economic tension for our kids such that they feel compelled to learn and grow?

This question has a lot in common with one that might at first appear wholly unrelated: *How do you hold the mind in meditation?* The suitable reply could be poetic, pithy, or atmospheric, and surely depends on the moment, the individual student, and what she/he needs. But one bit of meditation instruction never goes out of style. The mind should be held like this: *Not too tight, not too loose.* As to the matter of the young people and their finances, the analogy fits. We don't want to freak them out, nor do we want to support the misleading idea that one's financial life is just a bowl full of cherries. Sure, some cherries at the right time and in the right place are delightful. But that should not distract the young people from deepening their sense of responsibility for their journey. Meeting the economic challenges of life is a very real yoga for them. And it is our great privilege to guide them in this, be it by challenging them, or getting out of the way when they're doing fine by themselves, or recognizing the difference between us supporting them and enabling them in a given situation, or some combination thereof.

Our sense of how to create the right kind of economic tension for our kid will be nuanced. It will correspond to our kid's Type; and, it will be subtler than that. It doesn't get more personal. But let's go the other way for a moment, and head up to the Highly Capital Fiefdom of Greenwich, Connecticut, where all of this discussion of artfulness and attunement may matter little! Okay, that's unfair, since my swipe is based on a Sample of One. Still, I think the visit to the Land of Prep and Hedge Fund Managers could provide some comic relief, if not prove strangely useful in shining a light on this dynamic of economic tension.

IN THE QUEUE WITH SUZY Q

While visiting family in Rye a few years back, during that now unthinkable time when there was no Whole Foods in Port Chester, Maria and I had to motor several miles up the Boston Post Road to their store in Greenwich, to stock up on the special health, body, and food items that we felt we could not live without. In this feeling, we found we were not alone. It was a cold winter's day and the store was jam-packed with human beings pushing carts full of schtuffs and dressed in colorful garb. The fashion continuum went from super prep to the usual Patagonia, to bespoke business attire to the super chic. As for smiles on faces, I can't say there were many. Then again, I can't say that folks smile a whole lot while shopping in Whole Foods. Makes me wonder if I smile while shopping. I'll have to ask Maria. But I digress.

At some point the shopping cart was loaded up with our fair share of the American Dream, and now Maria and I stood in line for our turn to pay at the checkout counter. Chatting between ourselves, not watching our surroundings closely since we were on holiday, we at some point heard the murmurs of our fellow shoppers. Looking up, we saw that our checkout line had come to a complete standstill. Up at the register stood Suzy Q, a 16- or 17-year-old high school student who was half-blushing/half-pissed, and definitely avoiding all eye contact. Her phone was pressed to her ear and she had that look of *Come on, come on ... answer the phone.* Well, no one answered. The young woman hung up and turned back to the cashier—a woman in her fifties who reminded me of my Irish grandmother for some reason or other—and she pled her case:

"Please, believe me. There's no way my debit card balance is zero."

The cashier said in kind yet firm way, "I'm sorry; can't help you then, honey."

And the young woman, Suzy Q, raced out of Whole Foods empty handed, and the cashier called for assistance, to get someone to take the bag of groceries away from the counter, to put the stuff back on the shelf. It was all pretty bright, in a painful sort of way. But no one else in the line said a word about it, and I thought that was pretty odd. When it was our turn to check out, I said:

"Wow. That was too bad."

"What do you mean?," the cashier asked.

"You know, for that young gal to do her shopping and then not have sufficient funds in her debit card account."

"Oh, no," said the cashier. "That is a regular occurrence in these parts. Young person with a debit card, and an allowance. And when the money runs out, they all call Mom; and I gotta give Mom credit. She never answers the phone ... ever! I guess that's one way to keep a budget! When you're out, you're out!"

And she laughed a merry laugh, and moved on to the next customer.

As I walked away, kind of amused and definitely amazed, I thought to myself: *That's one way to unhitch from the roller coaster of your kid's running-out-of-funds drama.* I even had to admit I kind of liked the setup which lands some number of kids back on "ground zero." However, I also had to wonder whether these kids were learning anything besides: *This sucks! I want a bigger allowance.* I had my doubts. And I suspected that few meaningful conversations took place around these, shall we say, mini-crash landings. Hope I am wrong.

. . . .

It's a double-mirror question. It's a relational question. I broached it in Part One when contemplating Quixotic Caitlin's flights of fancy. It'll get broached again when, a few chapters thence, Maria recounts her experience of rolling up her sleeves and "working" in close with our daughter, Taia. For us all, this terrain is deeply personal. I don't know the answer. But I do know the question.

How do we as parents/guides "create" the right kind of economic tension for our kids, such that they feel compelled to learn and grow?

 # No Time Like the Present

If a kid hits ground zero with a small thud or big kaboom, but then has no one with whom to meaningfully process that experience, that is a great educational opportunity lost. Mistakes, as they say, are teachable moments; and, while that particular phrase irritates me to high heaven, I think it true in these instances. Thinking back to Suzy Q and the scene she made at the Greenwich Whole Foods, I hope she ultimately found herself on the receiving end of a firm, if not pointed, conversation with her mom or dad, the latter saying something like, "No, you won't be getting a bigger allowance. I don't care that Polly gets more than you. But, tell me, what did you learn about yourself? Your spending habits? About the fact that you spent your monthly allowance in two weeks?" I can't really comment beyond that since I don't know Suzy Q's family from Adam. However, I can say that IF her parents are consistently *in conversation* with her about Life & Its Money-Related Issues, then the educational benefits will tend to trend powerfully. Efficacy lies in the many small conversations. The grand lectures, by contrast, should generally be kept to a minimum. It's not just that they are unpleasant and thus get predictably tuned out by the person on the receiving end. They also miss the point that so much of what's going on here is the pedagogy of osmosis whereby our kid over time becomes familiar with the issues, the data points, and the basic language of money. Repetition should become everyone's friend. If it doesn't, or worse, if repetition becomes the Dread Parental Hammer, then it's time to reassess. Is our kid being a pill? Or, are we not succeeding in speaking the dialect of his/her ZM Type?

Chapter 28 **Taking Flight – Notes #1**

L et's put away the album of sweet Suzy Q testing the limits of home and high school life, and leap forward to the truly gritty time when our kid, in quintessential Whitman fashion, takes to the Open Road. Here, the stakes are high, certainly higher than zeroing out one's debit card account, and the audience watching isn't a bunch of disinterested strangers at Whole Foods, but us, the people who know and love, and at times bankroll, our kid. I right now am focused on the age 21 to 24 corridor, though this could take place before or after. The point is our kid seeks to make her move, to leave the home she grew up in and make it out there on her own. This act of "taking flight"—yes, we'll also make generous use of the popular fledgling metaphor—is exciting and chaotic. Nor does it end there. The ensuing period of flying economically low is a vulnerable and nervy time in its own right, and might last a year or two or three or longer. It might also include a small crash-landing or two, pit stops for refueling, and additional negotiations to refinance with JP Morgan, or, more likely, with the Bank of Mom & Dad. Suffice it to say, our role in this particular coming-of-age ritual is hardly written in stone. Some days, we're a part of the action. But, increasingly, we bear witness. This shift nevertheless does little to reduce the emotional intensity of what's going on. I myself can't help but think of the Wright Brothers at Kitty Hawk, testing variables, assessing, taking flight, catching air for long or short periods of time, and back to the drawing board, to tweak what needs tweaking. I like that analogy, the one that involves our kid on the hills of Kitty Hawk, NC. There, we watch the spectacle with eyes wide open and, when necessary, with eyes shut tight!

The field of play is also decidedly social. The surrounding social environs generate their own intense vibe. Setbacks for our kid can become more than personally embarrassing, to wit, they're often highly public. Ending up back in your childhood digs where George the Monkey lies on the bed and looks like he's been awaiting your return—well, that hurts plenty good, but then there's the world as witness. Neighbors, friends, and family members never seem to miss a beat, and they do like to talk. Their judgments likely are benign, especially when compared to the bizarre wizards of the 21st-century American media, who definitely have to get their chops in. Apropos taking flight and coming of age, the deployment of shaming narratives in the American media are still reliable money makers (i.e., yes, even the *NY Times*: "It's Official: The Boomerang Kids Won't Leave," and that's a relatively nice article), though speckled here and there are thoughtful writers with generous narratives. How these latter pieces manage to see the light of day, I don't know. Anyway, as of this moment, the American press doesn't seem too keen on this emerging generation of young Americans. Maybe the press bias expresses an institutional kind of ageism. I suspect it does, though maybe this isn't news at all. Maybe every older generation does this, inflicting its bias on the emerging, younger generation with an array of unflattering and facile labels.

Faced with this social clamor and the daunting nature of the leap itself, our fledgling kids will understandably have moments of self-doubt; and, we, in our role as parent, guide, and banker, may experience a slew of fear-based emotions ourselves. We might even feel impelled to act, to protect, to intervene and do the work for the kids, or try to make a deal with the gods or the devil on their behalf. As noted previously, that's what depth of love can make us do. But if at all possible we should go the other way. This is the time to seek counterweights to these inclinations, and work in *that* opposing direction, lest our love become cause for sabotaging the kids, our own finances, or both. So, as I offer you now my thoughts on Taking Flight and what it might mean for each of the ZM Types, I'll quite deliberately work in that counterbalancing direction. For, love is not diminished by rules or protocols or boundaries. Quite the opposite. Done well, I think these structuring elements bring supreme protection to us, our kids, their journey, and our wallet. How about I get things rolling with a story of one of my people.

THE GRADUATE

When my son, Mikyo, finished college, he and I drove the old Saab 9-3 the 2200 miles from Maine back to Boulder. It was the first week of June 2010. The days were hot as the hinges. The AC in the Saab was defunct, or so I'd learn within ten minutes of embarkation. I had forgotten how big America is, moreover. I used to make this trip all the time, between Rye, New York and Boulder, Colorado when I myself had been in college, but this time the road would unequivocally show that I wasn't that guy anymore! No worries, though. We had a sane plan. Four days of eight hours of driving would do the trick. No sleeping in rest areas, no living on coffee for 48 hours, no cruddy radio stations. We'd be civilized, even if the hot air snapped in our ears because the windows had to be down. We'd be sanguine, listening to Bach cello suites, Radiohead, and various incarnations of Jeff Tweedy. And we'd amuse ourselves, yelling stories both new and well worn above the din of wind. This was life along I-70, headed west, blurring across the swelter of the American heartland.

The elephant in the car was, well, impossible to miss: *What is the kid's next big life move?* But I let sleeping elephants lie. For starters, the kid was exhausted. He had kicked it out in classroom and in sport for four consecutive years. He had finished strong; so strong, in fact, that I could feel his adrenals were still pumping, even though finals had ended days before. And while he maturely delivered on his end of the college bargain, it was easy to see he was still the tender age of 21: All he could he think about was getting home, partying with his buds, sleeping late, taking long runs in the foothills, having the space to practice classical guitar or watch a movie. For our part, we, the parents, had no issue underwriting a month's worth of such festivities. The kid had earned it.

But the month of the victory lap was not to be. Once home, he learned his best buds were nowhere to be seen. One friend was in Amsterdam doing what inspired young Americans do in Amsterdam, while another was gone fishing for salmon in Alaska. Yet another was totally MIA, quite an accomplishment in this digital age. In that social void, however, Mikyo kept crossing paths in town with parents of friends. These interactions sounded innocent and sweet enough, but together they struck an odd and dissonant chord. It all set him to thinking in a fresh direction.

One night over dinner Mikyo mentioned there was a girl

in the picture—a beguiling young woman he'd fallen for right as school was ending. Now, isn't that the opening chapter of so many life stories: *There was a girl!* She was in Boston. Hmmm. It just so happened that a merry band of mates from college had also recently taken up residence there. Hmmm. Boulder seemed less and less like home. And then it all tipped. No surprise: The kid wanted to go to Boston.

Now the economics of the situation took center stage. He needed a job, and he needed a plan. For two weeks he worked the Boston job search as hard as he could from Boulder. The distance was a problem. I'll spare you the details but Mikyo made a compelling case for going to the source. To get a job in Boston he had to be in Boston. It was at this moment that I became quite swiftly his prospective banker! Things had to be done in the proper way. Only I had a clear idea of what that might mean. Over time, that would definitely change.

. . . .

Author Note: As it pertains to these personal accounts, I will often employ "me" and "I" in the telling, but please know that whatever is going on is the product of "we." I employ the first person for the sake of narrative flow, and because it sounds stronger. But beyond such rhetorical considerations, I should be emphatic in noting that all is inseparable from the (literal) *royal we.* This is no political correctness on my part. In terms of parenting-in-action, my wife, Maria, and I have repeatedly come together *on the big parental issues.* This is not to say that we have always begun in harmonious fashion. Hardly! But, as a matter of habit, we have

had the conversations, skirmished where needed, and generally hung in there till we both felt good enough, or quite positive
about the decision rendered. This commitment to "relationship
work" had done us well and was in force yet again.

Chapter 29 The Beantown Plan

You may recall that in the summer of 2010 the eurozone tried to implode (luckily, the matches were soggy), the American economy was smoking a big fat one (so named Quantitative Easing in *bankerese, man*), and businesses large and small, like the bees in Winnie the Pooh, were highly suspicious. Jobs? What jobs? No one was hiring. In light of that, was Mikyo daunted? Not particularly. Ah, the resilience of youth, where youth is not wasted on the young. This Song of the Open Road business was all systems go for Mikyo. I thus scrambled to sketch out some numbers ahead of time. And while it helped that I'm in the financial advisory business, I'm sure that—between talking with friends/family and mining the web—you could come up with some pretty good estimates of the cost of the launch on your own. The sum of my pencil-on-the-napkin tally was the kid would need a line of credit for 12k to 15k, in order to buy up to 6 months' time. That's not a lot of time to land a decent job. Nor is it a lot of money. But wait: It is a lot of money! It's real money, and it's my hard-earned money. After some contemplation, I felt quite clear that I only wanted to offer ONE of these lines of credit per kid, per lifetime.

Here is how I arrived at the estimated 12k-15k Line of Credit Calculation, followed by some notes on key choices Mikyo had to make regarding shoring up (or not) the income side of the equation. To restate: Mikyo would get one of these Lines of Credit per lifetime, so getting a part-time gig might be wise to slow down the "burn" rate and give him the longest possible time to find the Semi-Decent First Serious Job After College. Then again, such a strategy might split his energy and efforts, and be exactly the wrong move for him. Anyway, see the following:

Expenses (projected)

Rent	*1k/month for a room & utilities/internet*	1k/month
Rent	*One time deposits for 1st month & security*	2k (1x upfront)
Food	*$600/month*	.6k/month
Car	*Owned by Mikyo, no debt. Tires & basic mechanics of car OK. He'll live in the city. Travel minimal for a while.*	0
Car – Gas	*$100/month*	.1k/month
Car – Insurance	*We'd pay it for now*	0
Insurance Health	*We'd keep him on family plan for now*	0
Cell phone	*Family Plan, we'd pay it for now*	0
Meals & Entertain	*$300/month Keep it minimal. This is job search time. Meals, coffee, tea at home, occasional beer out. Occasional movie out.*	.3k/month
Transit in City	*$200 month taking the "T" and taxis*	.2k/month
Clothes	*We'd buy biz type clothes before he left*	0
Unexpected	*7% contingency rule*	.25k/month

Total projected for 1 month's ordinary expenses ························2.5k

Total projected for 4 months' ordinary expenses ······················10k

One-time initial costs (1st month's rent and security deposit) ··········· 2k

Launch capital remaining after 4 months – assume no income ··········3k

Income (three questions)

Mikyo began his journey, as noted, with a line of credit to pull from, plus a few bucks of his own in a savings account, but no income to speak of. Let's then consider three questions that arose. They were anticipatory in nature. I offered frames and ideas. The final decisions were necessarily his own.

#1: Should I get a part-time gig while pounding the pavement for the Semi-Decent First Serious Job After College? [7]

By the time Mikyo arrived in Boston, he needed an answer to this question of strategy. On the plus side, any part-time income would slow down the "burn rate," which, after excluding the rent deposits, was approximately $2.5k per month. On the negative side, holding down a part-time gig could become a terrible distraction, and zap him of critical time, energy, and focus.

My general comment to Mikyo was this, "I recognize this is an important question, but I can't say what the right answer is. You'll have to measure the risks and returns of Side Job v. No Side Job.

"Obviously, every little bit of income will buy you extra time in the big search. On the other hand, time is precious and being focused is critical to the ultimate goal. The decision is yours. The impact on the outcome is yours. It will have no bearing on the Line of Credit I offer you."

---

7 Of course your kid doesn't have be a grad of a four-year college. More think in terms of that age 20 to 24 time corridor.

After some contemplation and discussion, Mikyo decided to devote himself exclusively to the job search for two months; and, if it didn't look promising after that, he'd seek part time or temp employment, or perhaps even rethink his whole plan.

#2: What if the First Serious Job is within one's sights, and awesome, but the pay, not so much?
Weaving in and through this Anticipatory Planning Discussion was a thread about the hiring practices of some of the more *highly pursued employers*—a few of whom were on Mikyo's list. This group frequently offered newbies a foot-in-the-door part-time gig, aka a trial period, or a quasi-internship with modest pay, to see how things work out. Variation on this theme: Some of these companies made the full-time hire, but kept the pay low for the entry-level jobs. All the more was this phenomenon prevalent in a town like Boston where there's an oversupply of young talent in the labor pool.

Understandably, Mikyo wanted to know how I might come down on this, in the event that he received such an offer.

I myself was noncommittal though generally supportive. No, that doesn't make me a politician! Rather, I expressed the view that the chance to work at a visionary company with talented folks around might be just the ticket for him. I also took the opportunity to state that he might then need to make lifestyle choices, if not sacrifices, and be very disciplined with personal expenditure. A penny saved meant he'd have more economic staying power to get the remuneration side of things up to speed in his life. Beyond that, yes, he and I would huddle in such an instance of great gig, insufficient pay. More financial help might come from Maria and me. But make no mistake about it, we were middle-class people. We had a life and had to be smart with how we parted with our precious resources. Still, the door would be open. The purse might well open. If and when such a moment arrived I'd have to think about it long and hard, which is why at the outset I was generally supportive though noncommittal.

#3: If I seek a part-time gig, is one route better than another?
Returning to the subject of (perhaps) doing part-time work while steadfastly pursuing the Semi-Decent First Serious Job, I offered Mikyo this counsel, "If you find yourself needing a part time job to slow down your cash burn rate, then carefully consider what you want."

Here I bifurcate the field like this. There are the max cash/low visibility gigs v. okay cash/better visibility gigs. The former lead one straight to the service sector, i.e., waiting tables, tending bar, etc. Enhanced by cash tips, the pay can be very good, but the job itself probably won't provide much in the way of enduring *capital* benefits. Sure, it's possible to make a meaningful connection or two while on the job, or glean business skills that apply at the next level, but don't count on it. And this is no judgment on this physically active kind of work, especially as I've been there myself. For three years while in school in the eighties I worked as a barista at a café in Boulder. I appreciated the job, though I was always on my feet and thus pretty tired at the end of a shift. The people who frequented the café were decent, my co-workers fun and smart, the pay better than most comparable gigs. Of course, I wasn't out there looking for a serious full-time job; I was in school still. This is a critical distinction, and natural bridge to the other route. For, if making a connection or two is what Mikyo would be hoping for, or acquiring a special skill that could be used down the road, then I think it'd make sense for him to place himself in the center of a more formal work setting (i.e., clerical jobs, office admin, temp gigs, etc.). The trade-off, as mentioned, is that usually these jobs pay modestly, or worse. But ideally they'd also put him in circulation. No guarantees, of course. We've all heard the stories of death-by-filing or sorting mail in the mailroom by the hum of phosphorescent lights in windowless rooms. Great way to work on one's pallor and to perfect the art of talking to walls!

Anyway, the hope is that the office-type gig gives Mikyo or your kid a higher profile and/or puts him in circulation. Luck and probabilities now join forces. Or, as social scientists like to point out, most job leads come from co-workers, friends of friends, and friends of acquaintances; to wit, from the proverbial weak ties. Again, I offer no right answer here, nor guarantees, just the framing of another strategic decision that Mikyo or your kid might be called on to make.

Chapter 30 Old JP Morgan, Maria, & Me

Already, in the summer of 2010, it was on the table that we were proud of Mikyo as a person, of his accomplishments in school and sport and social life, and that we were ready to be supportive of him in his next life move. This was the love side of the equation. It explained why we were doing "business" together in the first place: Because we loved him, because he'd created a lot of good will that made it natural for him to ask for our support. **But love is the reason, not the ways and means.** Things still had to be done in the proper way. Values counted. We were middle-class people. I know I just asserted that, but it's worth repeating. In our house privileges were earned. Maria and I paid for two undergrad college educations (Taia's would come not long after Mikyo's) because we believed in education and because the kids had shown us they were serious about it, too. That's how it worked, and we were very upfront with them on this point. In many ways what Mikyo and I did with the Beantown Plan was an extension of that; we fashioned a revised *agreement*, a revised social and economic *contract*. Predicated on love and affinity and affection, this contract nevertheless contained some fine print, mostly in the form of a line-by-line budget, and some very real capital elements, which is to say, our line of credit had limits; don't count on a bailout. Terms of support got spelled out. Roles and responsibilities got clarified. It was an agreement that recognized Mikyo's agency, my agency, but also our interconnectedness. These terms were not separate from the journey. Indeed, to summon Whitman's words, they would become the delicious burdens that Mikyo would take with him as he set out, as he took to the Open Road.

Chapter 31 Taking Flight – Notes #2

Taking flight is a somewhat misleading phrase in that it could imply a one shot deal when, in fact, we're talking about a long runway, one if not several liftoffs, and then the extended period(s) of flying low. And, while taking flight is a definite achievement, it is only the end of the beginning: Our kids will fly low for a long time before they achieve something that resembles personal economic stability. Take a financial goal as basic as systematically saving to fund a cash backstop (you know, the "opportunity" or "rainy day" fund that we're all supposed to have in a high yield savings account to cover, say, six months of expenses in our life). Something as basic as that is not easy for our kids to accomplish right off. It may take them five years to stash away 10k. Or, just as easily and legitimately, they will choose not to; that is, those funds could get claimed for other "self-investment" items such as specialized education or any variety of tools, wardrobe, etc., or moving to another town to be closer to identified opportunities. To have very little savings as a cash backstop, or next to none, is what I mean by *flying low*. It's an intense aspect of the journey, and it can be a bit nerve-wracking to recognize that a small crash

could morph into a big setback. And to add some more wracking to our nerves, there's no uniform answer to what the "perfect" or optimal amount of economic tension is for the kids. Too
much tension and they won't perform well. Not enough tension
and they won't bother to deliberate on the trade-offs that go into
a decision well made. But even if just the right chord is struck,
the song remains the same: The vast majority of young people in
their twenties are flying awfully low for long periods of time. The
strain of this might leave some of them vulnerable to taking an
ill-advised short cut—i.e., one that flirts with the devil, aka taking
on credit card debt.

Given the easy availability of lines of credit from credit card
companies, and how such loans can bring an immediate sense of
freedom (to spend) or short-term relief from the constraints of a
situation, it's understandable how any person, whether young or
old, might fall prey to misusing them. This, we know, happens all
the time, and too often ends badly. The Old Fart in me says: No
one should be allowed to get a credit card without first passing
some kind of financial literacy test. If only! Anyway, the storyline
gets pulled taut in the oft-recounted Hemingway gem in *The Sun
Also Rises*. In witty fashion, Hemingway points to the evil of cas-
cading, compounding debt when, in response to his American
friend's query, the very affable Englishman (Bill) declares how in
fact he went bankrupt: *Gradually and suddenly!*

No truer words.

Trouble has a way of starting innocently. Then it builds, and
builds powerfully, because of the negative compounding effect.
That is, one falls behind and increasingly pays interest not only
on the original amount borrowed, but on the interest itself. Ow!
Actually make that Double Ow!, because digging out from the
negatively compounding, high interest rate debt avalanche is ex-

ceedingly difficult and can therefore become a major distraction on the Open Road journey. It also presents the family system with a truly un-fun quandary: To bail out, or not to bail out, Little Johnny Appleseed?

GOING HEAVY ON YOU

I'm going to keep my counsel here simple and direct, and confined to the preventative side of things. I recommend we address early and often this issue of credit card use and misuse, starting around the time our kid goes to college and then into The Agreement post-college. *You want my financial support in and through college, or as you take flight in your own life, then do not accumulate credit card debt. If you use a credit card, pay it off IN FULL each month. This isn't a demand: It's a requirement. Adhere to it and in this domain I will trust and respect you. Violate this agreement and there will be trouble.* But beyond abiding by the rules, there is a core challenge implicit in all of this. That is: *Learn to be financially honest in your life.* In 21st-century America, with the myriad seductions of consumerism mixing with how people (understandably) wish to feel larger and more arrived or more beautiful than perhaps they are—well, all of this conspires to make being financially honest one of the most difficult things to consistently do.

IN OUR TIME

Whether or not I've succeeded, I meant to strike a kind of rugged, Rocky Mountain moral tone. At the same time, I must say I don't buy all that malarkey linking weakness of character to financial mismanagement. It is terrifyingly easy to live beyond one's means, and good kids (and good folks) do it all the time. Exactly who is going down this rabbit hole, and when, is hard to say, but it's safe to assert that almost every day we're surrounded by this financial madness. It's the shadow side of what is perhaps the most agreed-upon social construct of our time: *Consumerism.* Think about it. In a time when there is a preponderance of ugly culture clashes, when America looks more like several disparate countries as opposed to "One nation, under God, indivisible …", it certainly seems to me like these otherwise diverging Parties agree on one thing, namely, the robust consumption of quality material goods and a wide variety of curated experiences. I mean no sanctimony. I've got my spiffy golf clubs in the back of my groovy car; I dependably incline toward my preferred travel habits; and I think highly of my ideas for fun, getting together with family and friends, being a foodie, and so on—most all of which cost money and to a degree pay homage to the gods of our consumer culture. Perhaps one day we'll all drink out of a punch bowl spiked with something else (i.e., more Nature and fewer things?, more spirit of mutuality and less "me" and "my"?); but, until then, I will drink from the punch bowl of American consumerism and individualism, and, yes, I will attempt to drink responsibly just like the beer commercials on television advise me to do.

I say this with humility, for I'm a social animal, after all. And while I may have a healthy sense of self, and continue to be something of a goddamn independent whether I like it or not, none of that precludes my need to socially belong, nor does it extinguish my periodic desire to win the esteem of my family, friends, and community. Whether the current consumeristic punchbowl party can be supported by the planet for much longer—well, yes, let us all figure out the next collective move. The obstacle surely isn't consumption itself. Some of that is fine and quite necessary.

Rather, it's the disentangling of identity issues/social status from material things/consumer brands. Can we have a strong sense of self without all of our material markers to tell the world who we are? As well, will the world know who we are, and will we know who we are, if we don't adorn ourselves with our favorite things/brands?

Arguably, the most powerful effect of consumerism (delivered via advertising) is how it subtly shapes and colors our ideas about what it is to look sexy, successful, cool, and beautiful. I could write volumes on this point, though many people cleverer and more learned than I have done just that. Besides, my objective here is less ambitious. I prefer to remind us how very human we are and how vulnerable we can feel. All the more is this true for the young people whose brain neural wiring may not be complete and whose sense of identity may not be firmly established. These kids, namely our kids, are particularly susceptible to falling for the nicely packaged prescriptions that promise so much. Then add in the factor of readily available credit. It greases the wheels and makes the *false acquisition* of so many of these things and experiences dangerously easy. For, who isn't attracted by the social payoffs of a cool car, a sweet apartment in sweet neighborhood, the teal colored Steve Madden boots, or a sparkly outfit that surely belongs to Venus? He/she gets to look like a million bucks, and, everybody says so, and yes, these payoffs prime the limbic pump in our kid's brain. In the moment of truth, then, when the *voice of financial honesty* might tell Johnny or Caitlin to decline the invite to beers with friends or dinner at the trendy restaurant (because it ain't in the budget), these very powerful and pleasurable payoffs may prove too much.

Offsets are essential, therefore, to cool things down, to bring the right kind of friction to otherwise well-lubricated situations that give the marketplace (and one's peers) a huge advantage over our kid. To come are but a few ideas of my own. I encourage you to use them as a springboard to creating your own ideas. That sort of adaptability seems like the necessary response (from us) to the genius and fast-changing manipulation of media players who know how to create demand for a product or experience better than the sun knows how to shine. In many ways I'm talking about the needs v. wants issue. The genius of the American media & advertising machine knows how to blur those lines. It's our task to un-blur them and wake up that sharp, discerning quality in our kid.

 Love Strikes Back

It is essential to help our kids see through the seductions of *I want* and *I must have,* seductions and distortions that the American consumeristic machine incessantly and dazzlingly manufactures. We, as guides and parents, aspire to level the playing field for our kids, before their confusion deepens. We want them to take care, not only for themselves and their wallet, but for us, too. This is what love can make us do: Take care in beautiful and conscientious and enduring ways. I'm thinking in particular of our kids increasingly deciding to take care. Sure, there will be forgetting and alternation and episodes of monkey business, but ideally our kids will know True North and repeatedly return to the light of love and honor and loyalty and care and integrity. Perhaps paradoxically, it is due to the strength of these emotional ties, these emotional "assets," that I strongly recommend that at some point along the way we get into the habit of being quite formal in our dealings that have an economic component and, when appropriate, even make a written Agreement with our kid.

The emotions are perhaps the most powerful driver in the life of human beings. Madison Avenue knows this. The Buddha knows this. Why shouldn't we ride this train, too? In our case, we're focused on what might be described as the well-favored emotions; that is, the emotions of love and friendship, *and* the emotions that spring from there. Time then to mobilize these forces. Time then to deploy them as powerful offsets. To my mind: Only the conscious mustering of these relational energies will give our kid a fighting chance in the myriad moments of financial truth. In many ways this is what we're doing when we go formal and make an Agreement with our kid. We invoke gravitas. We memorialize in writing the intergenerational meeting of hearts and minds. Some observers might see this as the clarion call to integrity. Others might see this as turning up the volume of the superego voice. Either way, the efficacy lies in using the emotions themselves (i.e., love, honor, care, integrity) to seal the deal. Yes, seal the deal. We're doing this deal because we love our kid; and, no two ways about it, we expect that kind of love in return. We expect honor and care and integrity from them. We expect them to take personal responsibility for their journey. This kind of heavy offset is quite necessary. *Am I doing the right thing? Am I being financially honest? Am I honoring the Agreement I made with myself and my folks?*

Passion and impulse quicken the thought process, and that can spell trouble when action follows at full tilt. We instead want to slow things down. Again, that's what we're doing in the Agreement process: We are creating a relationship-centric offset. Now our kid *aspires* to take as much responsibility for the relationship with us as we are with him. If he veers off, and surely from time to time he will, then we remind him of this loving and intense ground of mutuality. For the journey is his own, but it's also incumbent on him to increase his awareness of how his choices impact the close-in relationships that enrich his life. Being independent includes tuning into the greater family and social ecosystem. Being autonomous includes learning the art of inter-dependence.

WORLD IN A PHRASE

Let me suggest two additional moves that also specifically aim to undermine the enormous pull of consumerism. Compared to the heavy offset of The Agreement, they're light and airy, and rely on the turn of a phrase; actually, two phrases. First: *That's not in my budget.* And, second, whether in response to another person or a specific impulse to act or buy: *Maybe, yes. Maybe, no. I need to look at my budget first.* I know, such lyrics clearly aren't pilfered from Radiohead or the Rolling Stones, and appear to have more in common with the *Book of Soils.* Even so, they work! Their efficacy lies in how simple they are to grab in the moment of truth. And the moment of truth, as noted before, is usually pretty darn challenging. Friends and family members (like peer cousins, or siblings) can apply pressure on the kids to do things beyond their means or to push them to present themselves in ways that really are a financial stretch, and in such moments our twenty-something kids can feel like they're back in junior high succumbing to peer pressure. To be sure, it's not all out there. The kids can do a number on themselves, and on us, too. So, the two budget-infused phrases also have self-application. They can help our kids ward off pressures born of that very human wish to be more ________________ than they currently are.

That's not in my budget!
or:
Maybe yes, maybe no. I need to look at my budget first.

These pieces of verbal/cognitive armor only work, however, if one already has a budget in place. A real budget. A real, unsexy, unpoetic budget that honestly reflects the cost of one's life. Then something else can take root. It has to do with the earthy goodness of being committed to being financially honest in one's life, and in fact mostly living by that code. It's an incredibly good feeling that is realizable for all the young people, whether Archer or Architect or Maven or Creative. And this brings me to my final note on the topic: While it is doubtless true that Creatives and Architects will benefit the most from this moderate though pithy form of mind training, and while it's likely the case that they'll need to practice these lines a number of times in the mirror before it is theirs, let's also remember to equip the young Archers and Mavens with these handy phrases. They need to be empowered, too, to know that "no" and "maybe" and "budget" are, if not cool, then at least intelligent words to say. Indeed, their autonomy on the open road of life depends on it.

  Taking Flight – Notes #3

L et's keep on with the budget groove. In the summer of 2010, through a series of strange coincidences, Mikyo landed a job within weeks of his arrival in Boston. I'm aware that sometimes real life sounds terribly implausible; I'm also aware that even the best of parents can in moments be insufferable braggarts. I myself think dark thoughts when someone waxes on and on about how lucky he's been in life. As if! In my own life it's been a mixed bag. In moments I've been luckier than perhaps I deserved, but, equal and opposite, I've also magnetized my share of un-luck, too. As for Mikyo, his was a curious start to the Open Road journey. It began before he had even left Boulder. He and I were running around town doing last minute errands, since he was leaving for Boston the next day. It was a ferociously hot summer afternoon, so we took some shade in the Trident Café in west Boulder and we grabbed a beverage and cooled off. While sitting there in a bit of daze, in walked an old college buddy of mine. Billy had been living down in Denver for a number of years and I never seemed to see enough of him. But here we were. There were more strange details connecting Bill and Mikyo (the image of Mikyo at the age of 3 dressed like a little man as a guest at Bill's wedding comes to mind, or how Bill attended two colleges for undergraduate work—the same two colleges that Mikyo and I respectively attended), but I'll spare you the longer list. Anyway, Billy hadn't seen Mikyo in years and, pleasantries being what they are, he asked Mikyo what he was up to. Mikyo gave the thumbnail sketch of his Beantown plan, and Billy responded with a burst: He had a brother, Steve, in Boston, and Steve ran a company, and, well, Mikyo would just have to look him up. *It can't hurt!* A few weeks and two thousand miles of driving later, Mikyo paid a visit to Steve in Boston, hoping to share a bit about his job-search interests and gather whatever intelligence or connections he could. But Steve liked Mikyo right off, and had him stick around the shop for about four hours that day, and at some point Mikyo worried that he had overstayed his welcome, and that's when Steve said he wanted to offer Mikyo a job as an analyst.

Crazy.

Still, before signing on the dotted line, there was one rather essential matter in need of sorting: Compensation. Steve & Company didn't make a specific offer; rather, they asked Mikyo what he was looking for. Since this was a first-ever Serious Job offer and since Mikyo hadn't seen such an offer coming from this introductory visit, Mikyo said he'd need to noodle on the compensation question and get back to them in the next day. Then my cell phone rang. *Did not see that coming. Got a job offer from Bill's brother. What should I ask for in the way of compensation?* Mikyo grabbed his laptop in Boston and I grabbed mine in Boulder, and we opened the latest iteration of the spreadsheet with the Beantown budget on it. At the very least, or so the logic went, Mikyo should be paid a wage that covered the cost of living in Boston. Below is what the budget looked like *after* we revised it from pre-launch/bare-subsistence lifestyle to the time of post-launch/flying low.

Mikyo living in Cambridge

LINE ITEM	LOW BALL	MID BALL	HIGH BALL	NOTES AS OF 8.22.2010
Rent	950	950	950	*rent due on the 1st*
Utilities	93	93	93	*landlord bills monthly*
Parking	15	15	20	
Food	300	300	350	*160 per month + incidentals*
Gas	320	320	360	*2 full tanks per month*
Public Transport				
Auto Repair	200	200	200	*250 per quarter*
Auto Tires				*rotate tires/new every 2 years*
Auto Insurance	100	100	100	*payment every 6 months*
Eating Out	200	300	400	*micro analysis to be done*
Going Out (Drinks)	150	225	300	
Events (sports,music)	100	130	160	
Fees	100	100	100	
Fines	60	60	60	*parking ticket(s)*
AT&T Service	100	100	110	
Rhapsody	10	10	10	
iTunes	25	38	50	
Miscellaneous	66	75	100	*coffee, tea, snacks*
Household	20	25	30	
Clothes	50	50	50	*clothing-needs convo*
Gym	50	50	50	
Taxes	*TBD*	*TBD*	*TBD*	*fed & state—not sure*
MONTHLY	$ 2,909	$ 3,140	$ 3,492	
YEARLY	$34,908	$37,680	$41,904	

Base Salary Needed *(with 26% tax-rate added)*

	$43,984	$47,477	$52,799

With 2K IRA contribution

	$45,984	$49,477	$54,799

Anticipated annual bonus *$1500*

*NOTE: 26 paychecks,
not 24, needs to be factored
into monthly cashflows.
Discuss with Mikyo.*

Life in Boston, without getting wild, though living in a nice part of town and putting 2k a year toward savings, meant that he'd need to be paid 46k gross per year. It'd be tight, but if it was a cool gig and he learned a lot, it'd be well worth the tight fit. Mikyo went back to Steve & Company, and asked for 44k/year and some health insurance benefits. He said this would cover his Boston life and that soon he hoped to make at least a couple thousand more so as to begin funding a savings goal. *Yes!* came the reply. Steve added that over time there certainly would be bonuses if they liked Mikyo's work. *Deal!*

· · · · · · ·

Speaking of grooves, here's Webster getting all definitional on us.

budget [*buj'it*] noun
1. an estimate of income and expenditure for a set period of time: *keep within the household budget* | [as modifier] :
a budget deficit.

ORIGIN late Middle English: from Old French bougette, diminutive of bouge 'leather bag,' from Latin bulga 'leather bag, knapsack,' of Gaulish origin. Compare with bulge. The word originally meant a pouch or wallet, and later its contents.

  # Financials Are Your Friend

When an aircraft pilot, while flying, enters dark storm clouds that prevent him from seeing the horizon or the ground, he experiences a phenomenon known as "spatial disorientation." His senses are no longer guided by the normal points of reference, and as a result he can no longer be sure which way is up or down. His perceptions are unreliable.

The only way a pilot can overcome spatial disorientation is to completely trust his cockpit instruments to tell him what is real. This is why student pilots are required to learn to fly their planes by instruments alone. This skill will save the pilot's life, especially when visibility is low.

. . . .

Before Mikyo set off for Boston, I was blunt in my communication about how the credit cards were to be used. Would I be checking up on him? No, not in the sense that I needed to see credit card statements every month. But I would from time to time ask him point blank if he was running a balance there, and I was not above doing the occasional spot check—i.e., *send me a PDF of the recent credit card statement*. Obviously, I expected him to be honorable in his communications to me, and he was. This also proved indispensable in bringing real time financial information to the fore. Six months later he had zero credit card debt, but he had burned through about 3K of his own 6K of savings. What was going on?

LOVE IN THE TIME OF THAI FOOD

There are different ways to track actual spending. None of them is especially smooth. Quicken is a weird and at times finicky program. Quickbooks is nice and all, but overkill for just tracking spending. Mint.com is pretty good, but it won't give you printable/savable reports. I myself have tried a number of approaches, and settled on the Quarterly Old School Approach (QUOSA). It goes like this. I know what my budget says my monthly nut is and I multiple it by 3. Let's say it's 10k per month, so my quarterly budget is 30k. Then my wife and I lay out 3 months of bank statements. For us, and for most folks, all expenses, and that includes the payment to the credit card company, get paid through that account. So my process begins like this:

Month 1 - Start Balance:	$10,000
Month 1 - End Balance:	$11,000
Month 1 - Total Deposits:	$12,000

Now we do the tally:

Start Balance (10k) plus Income (12k), minus End Balance (11k)

$$10k + 12k = 22k \qquad 22k - 11k = 11k$$

In Month 1, we spent 11k.

Then we do the same thing for Month 2 and Month 3. And, again for illustration purposes, let's say that we spent 12k in Month 2 and 12k in Month 3. In other words, our budget for that quarter (3 months) was 10k x 3 or 30k, but we actually spent 11k + 12k + 12k = 35k and this put us 5k over our budget. That's quite an overspend for a three-month period of time, though on occasion this happens; and, when it does, we then dig into the detail. We grab credit card statements and the check register and figure out if, a) something unexpected happened, b) we had a big expense that will flatten out over a period of time (i.e., tuition for a semester of college paid all at once), or c) we were simply out of control in one way or another.

My point in going through this tedium now with you is to say that this is the gritty scutwork of personal financial management, and it must be done. What's more, it can be done. Doing it Old School is fine; doing via Mint is fine; but it must be done—not all the time, but periodically. I'd recommend once a quarter. And now we return to Mikyo and our shared inquiry into what clearly was a $500/month overspend. What gave? Well, he'd be doing the scutwork and then we'd discuss his findings. And it came down to two budget lines that heretofore hadn't been fleshed out.

One was the very real cost of courting a young woman in a gender-traditional manner. I don't care to weigh on matters of gender and courtship in the greater American culture. To my mind these matters are deeply personal. Perhaps not a big surprise: I felt very supportive of Mikyo's preference to pay for as much fun and games as he could when he and Katie were out on the town. Cost of Mikyo's side of said courtship activity: $250/month. I discussed it with Maria, and we agreed to chip in $250/month for the next 12 months, at which time we'd revisit the matter.

The other budget-busting line was less charming. Working

long hours, usually getting home at 8pm or so, Mikyo had developed a habit for Thai takeout, to the tune of $250/month! Impressive, I know, but this line item he himself would have to remedy. Maria offered Mikyo some strategies for end of day, I-feel-wiped-out meal ideas, and asked if he'd like a Crockpot for the pork shoulder slow cook side of life, and Mikyo readily accepted the Crockpot and the recipes. Where it went from there I don't really recall, but Mikyo got back on track. And this reminds me to say a word about the second financial document that he and I would periodically update: The Balance Sheet. For, it had been while updating the Balance Sheet that it was clear for all to see that what had been 6k of savings at the credit union had now become 3k. That was what tipped us off to the overspending. It was also the ritualized moment (i.e., we were working the program) for him to report whether there was a balance on his credit cards—ideally, as noted, zero.

Balance Sheet–Mikyo Update 3/21/11

Assets	9/22/10 Value	Present Value
Car–Saab 9-3	$4000	$4000
Checking	$1800	$1800 *lowest balance each month*
Savings	$6000	$3000
Rent Deposit & Security		$2000

Liabilities		
Car Loan	0	0
Student Loan	0	0
Credit Card Balance (*Visa*)	0	0

Line of Credit from Mom and Dad		
Amount Used	($6000)	
Amount Remaining (Potentially)	$6000	

Since Mikyo was true to his Archer form, this was the first and last time we needed to address what had become his far-too-frequent ritual of getting Thai takeout. Even so, it was a great and very necessary process that he had to go through. Thai takeout wasn't in his budget, and Maria and I certainly weren't going to pay for it, and he got the message loud and clear. Next! And that is how Archers learn and grow, by the by. They're not all perfect. Rather, they're human beings who, once fully engaged, are keen students of the financial game. True enough, they're perhaps complicated in other domains of their life, but money—if they apply themselves to learning about it amidst their journey—isn't one of them.

. . . .

Let's call it a day regarding Mikyo and his Archerly journey—a journey that can make the rest of us in the family kinda jealous of how quickly he learns and integrates financial matters, not that that ever keeps us from loving him to pieces—and, instead, let's check in on my much beloved and very willful daughter, Taia T. Butler, and see what's going on. Last we looked, Taia had burned through her childhood savings in a 30-month burst while in college, and for her final semester of college she was headed home to live with Maria and me. This return of Taia to our abode naturally gave rise to a new accord. If Taia kept her fiscal (and spending) house in order, Maria and I would put aside the cash saved from not paying rent in the last semester and use it to match the money she earned (and saved) during that fall. Seeing as Taia only had a couple classes left to complete her degree and seeing as her prospects for working part-time and earning decent cash looked good, this was a pretty sweet opportunity for Taia to get back on the right side of things. Fortunately, this was not lost on Taia, or so her actions would bear out.

But really, there's another story, a story within the original Taia story that is in need of telling. It's complex as a double mirror. This is to say, sometimes we look at our kid and, instead of seeing him or her, what we mostly see are our own hopes, dreams, fears and limitations. This psychological phenomenon is hardly news, nor is it automatically neurotic. Freud and Jung referred to it as psychological projection. It's about as human as human can be. And it's something we, especially in close relationships, are constantly dealing with. How to clearly see the ones we love, beyond our projections and unconscious biases that may or may not fit them? It plays the other way, too. How can they see us clearly, and not get stuck in old parent/child assumptions about what's going on? At times it can all get exhausting. Financial matters have been known to provoke deep emotions, and some of those emotions have been known to quite mischievously move to the edge of, if not just out of the field of our awareness. Same goes for watching our kid come of age. There is depth of love, unbearable love, and we deeply wish to see our kid become an authentic individual, which is a kind of freedom for him or her. Meanwhile, these serpentine emotions, lurking on the edge or just out of the reach of awareness, can shape the course of events. Strangely, we all know this and yet it nonetheless happens. Very challenging, yet also inspiring! And, with this as my prelude, I, as narrator, step aside.

For, the story is not mine to tell. I wasn't in it with Taia the way that Maria was. On a slew of financial matters going back to age fourteen, Maria and Taia worked closely together. Yes, some sparks did fly. That's all in the game. But there were also some great moments of collaboration, with Taia bringing her

Architect/Planner mind to bear on some of Maria's purchasing decisions and Maria bringing her Maven/Implementer mind to bear on some of Taia's purchasing decisions (and, of course, life decisions). No, they weren't two peas in a pod. No, they weren't sisters. No, they weren't equals, much as there was great affinity and affection between them. So, yes, this is another reason why this is not my story to tell. There are the red and golden threads of a mother/daughter relationship that weave through this financial education story, and that must be told from the inside.

I believe it was right for me to discuss in some detail how Mikyo and I worked together. I was the primary parent on that one. But this time round, Maria, in relationship to Taia, was the primary parent. Why we did the father/son and mother/daughter configuration I can't say, and I'm not necessarily prescribing it. It's just how it played out for us. It's just what worked for us. Anyway, it is to Maria that I pass the talking stick. I myself am looking forward to the story within the story. Without further ado, here's Maria.

Chapter 35 **Maria's Song**

When I was a girl, our dog, Heidi, a German Short-haired Pointer, had no rules. She stole bread from Mrs. French's counter (brought it home in its bag), and scattered Colonel & Betts Custers' trash all over their yard. My mom received wrathful phone calls from these perturbed neighbors (and one time, in a fit of fury, Betts threw her trash all over *our* yard, which was kind of exciting in its own way), but in spite of all that, there was never any progress on this rules front for Heidi. She was still allowed to lick our plates after dinner. It was only right; she was so cute! We did at least give her the middle name of Trouble. That sure taught her a lesson.

Did I mention that mine was a Waspy upbringing? At Christ's Church, where we went maybe every other year on Christmas Eve, the minister would invariably talk in loving terms about his Golden Retriever. I'm sure there was wisdom embedded in the sermon, but it all sounded a lot like life with Heidi, and the Episcopalian congregation delighted in these outrageous, silly stories of misbehavior. We enjoyed a hearty chuckle on Jesus' birthday, before returning home to open presents (the Scandinavian tradition in our home).

I come from astoundingly good stock—Mt. Holyoke, Choate, Princeton, Parsons, and it was hoped that I would marry someone famous—like John Updike's kid, or, at the very least, the son of one of those nice Rye families. Must say, for a while I tried to like those fellows—I really did. But the heart is a crazy thing, and somehow Mother Nature in all her mischief knows that it's not a bad idea for different clans to mix it up. She says it's healthy. So, as it went, I chose an Irish Catholic boy from the other side of the tracks (as they say), where folks who were successful in the merchant world became *nouveau riche*, or at least that's what was whispered. This means they knew nothing of Old Money, which of course must be the best kind of money, except, wait! We're not supposed to talk about money at all! It's tacky and unrefined and, well, just forbidden. Bad stuff all around. Better to have good taste and leave it out completely.

So, with this incongruity in mind, personal money is a pretty funny interest (and possible obsession) of mine. That, along with death. I love digging up matters not meant for discussion, and I like to think that I have such an abundance of good taste that perhaps I'm allowed this bit of recklessness. But I do remember this: Back when I told my mom about Mark's first book, *Zen Money Blues*, of which I was an editor, she cautioned me quite strongly to not mention any kind of family finances in there—specifically *our* family finances.

Now, this would have been hard to do, since to this day I know next to nothing of my family-of-origin's finances. Top secret. In present life, my brother and I have had a sum total of three finance conversations with Dad, aka Svend, the sword-wielder of Mark's 7th Avenue mishap. Steve and I have asked specific questions, but have been privy to only bits and pieces, in case we suddenly come down with a bad case of greed and stop working altogether so as to fully devote ourselves to the serene anticipation of our inheritances. Which may or may not exist. Thank goodness we have no idea—who knows what hedonism could ensue?

Back in the day, when I was coming of age, there was zero discussion of money in my family, and, as a Maven ZM Type, my main strategy for feeling like a grownup was to have very few needs, spend little, and to make my dad proud by being frugal. Steve was braver than I, having been an unremorseful spender in his adolescence, which I did appreciate, since it paved the way for me and my halo. Dad thought Steve was irresponsible, which he was, but when I ponder those three recent, fruitless finance conversations, I fear that we both are still getting punished for this, at the ripe ages of 60 (him) and 56 (me). Naturally, we're damned either way, because broaching finance matters with our genteel parents never fails to make us sound money-grubbing, or desperate, or, the worst thing: Ungrateful. So much smarter to pretend money doesn't exist.

Given this dignified backdrop, perhaps my particular set of contradictions will make sense in relation to my willful, spender/planner Architect Type daughter, Taia. Let me dial it back to the years when I first related to her in terms of money, when Taia was a young teen, and Mark was busy developing the *Zen Money Blues* typology. We knew at that point that Taia was a Planner (Architect), since the sparkly rollout of holiday celebrations was her forte. Even May Day! My forte was simplicity and doing nothing (in that very excellent zen way of doing nothing), so Taia's style was the perfect complement. She knew how to make fun happen, and was devil-may-care in the money department—all of which was positively medicinal (for me) at that point in the game. She taught me how to shop for clothes (yup, I kept us in the budget), go to Red Rocks concerts, and plan mom/daughter trips to various mountain towns and even New York for some culture (my idea on the culture). Whenever we'd shop or travel, I brought my frugality along (hard not to since it's part and parcel of my Maven DNA), and I actually thought that my chops in smart spending were rubbing off on Taia. I thought she was learning something, there, and that she *got* the transmission around joyful thriftiness. Consignment stores could be fun too! I thought it was that easy.

Fast-forward now to Taia's college years, and the credit card disaster, and Maria's complete and utter paralysis. Not pretty, and I'm very mixed about sharing it all with you, but I'm going to trust that hearing about my ignorance will make you feel better about any of your less than stellar moments. So, let's unpack this hairy mess, with a little 20/20 hindsight. And, by the way, the only reason I agreed to write this chapter is that the ending of said four-year-long ignoring spell is a happy one. And I'm sure it's good for my journey to remember it in all its ugly detail, kind of like writing down an embarrassing dream.

It all started in a sneaky sort of way, when Taia was beginning college, and in no time she very smartly began playing right into my bigger-than-life fears that she might not be happy (or safe) if she didn't have free reign with my credit card. Each month when the bill came, and I broke into a body sweat, we'd have a serious meeting. I'd get all stern and scorpionic, and Taia would explain. In fact, she was a master at making a case for her many expenditures, so much so that I weirdly agreed to pay for about half of them. The other half would come out of her savings. I was sure this penalty would have serious impact, since, as a Maven, spending my own savings is worse than sticking pins in my eyes. But for Taia, it was about as impactful as giving her the middle name

Trouble (don't worry—that's not her middle name, but you get the point). For the Architect Type, dollar amounts and savings numbers just don't mean that much. The discomfort of decreasing funds doesn't register particularly … that is until those funds are all gone. We could say I wasn't using my noggin in terms of what might skillfully cause her some appropriate pain (seeing as how I already had inside info around her typology). But god forbid my girl might not be happy in her college years. I had drunk the punch of permissiveness, oddly sweet as it was.

What the hell was this girl buying, you ask? Well, you name it: Stuff to decorate her room, snacks for when she missed meals, party supplies for get-togethers with her new friends, fresh outfits and shoes for said parties, iTunes (millions of songs—who has time to listen to so many songs?), gas for road-trips, meals out, and the list goes on. In contrast, I was living like an Amish woman.

So we did this dance, month over month, year over year, and I flourished (in a nauseating sort of way) in the role of Taia's cover-up agent when Mark would ask questions at our quarterly household finance meeting (or when he'd plug in for the occasional come-to-Jesus meeting with Taia). I'd make a big deal of her reimbursements to us from her savings, and then swiftly move on to other topics. Seems I had some chops in the equivocation department myself; something to do with apples and trees, as Mark would say.

But before I detail the blessed moment in which I got my act together, let's dig even deeper into the *What Was Going On* question—for yours truly. Recently I was reading about a young gal who started a business after having been a stay-at-home mom for the duration of her children's younger years. Her business has to do with providing a place where grownups can delve into arts and crafts, since using our hands to make things (these days) is virtually (no pun) a lost art. In the interview about her newfound passion, she stated quite simply something like this: *Even though I loved every minute of being a mom, I needed to recognize that, in the process of raising my kids, I had completely lost myself! Now I'm able to remember who I am through pursuing my passion.*

This whole construct of losing one's self versus finding one's self struck me as the core issue beneath that tiresome war between women who are at home with their kids and those who choose to work—and let's not forget those who do something in between. The career women are always holding it over the at-home women's heads that they don't have a self (*you must be so bored!*), whereas the at-home gals are quick to point out to the career gals (via knowing smirks) that their own full-time parented kids are way better adjusted, blah, blah, blah. And, as a quick non sequitur: So far I'm observing that the new generation of young parents are not engaged in this battle, because they're just one heck of a lot more creative and free than we thought we were— and the dads are right in there as parenting partners. Very cool.

Anyway, back to the empty-nest mom (that'd be me), asking herself, *Who am I, anyway?*, with the awkward echo of the boomer generation of women who fought so hard to liberate themselves from such nonsense. I was pretty sure that I had not a single issue around having a sense of my Self, having attended an all women's college, having been a school-owner and educator over the years, and having been the granddaughter of one grandmother who attended my alma mater, Mt. Holyoke, and another (my willful German grandma), who attended Parson's School of Design—all this back in the 1920's. Now those were spunky women! Didn't *they* have a Self? Wasn't I exempt from such foolish introspection since they'd already forged the way?

But the irritating detail in my own path is this telltale four-year permissive bender, one which was surely getting in the way of my own pursuits of passion (since that's what I was supposed to be doing, after all). Instead, I spent an awful lot of time worrying about Taia, and simultaneously having no rules around money. I was connecting no dots whatsoever, which is weird for a relatively smart cookie whose career passion was none other than the Montessori method, which hangs its hat on healthy independence for the child. Crap! For some reason, I was perfectly fine with this ongoing problem, and my cluelessness as to how to solve it. Was I getting something out of this crazy rollercoaster? Did I secretly feel mixed about my very own daughter becoming her own person, and not needing me quite so much?

Another thread that I can't possibly disregard, even though I want to: The class-issue undertones of my Waspy upbringing. One piece of the shame game that happens from the stay-at-home mom toward the career mom is this unsaid assumption that the at-home mom is somehow better because she is financially able to not work, and that surely if the career mom had a choice, she would most certainly stay home. Isn't this what the liberated woman strives to do? To *choose* to stay home? So, it follows that the career gal must be of slightly lesser ilk than the home gal (how many times did I hear the word "ilk" growing up?). It's that thing about having a pure breed dog. Though, I'd argue that the mutt is so much healthier in all respects … but do let me gently back away from the imminent political overtone, here. That's not where I'm going.

Here's the deal. When I look back, I'm ready to call myself out on this one shocking point: I felt mixed about my daughter having to shoulder any financial burden or tension. I was subtly encouraging her to have expectations of one day becoming a Lady of Leisure. Yup, you heard that right; this is some major residue, people! And, while I did have a wonderful teaching career, I must admit to having chosen a career without a single thought as to whether I could help to support our family in a financially meaningful way. Not-for-profit institutions are exactly that—*sans* profit. It's kind of like taking up pottery or, even better, horseback riding. Might as well be playing the lute.

Now that I've gotten that off my chest, I'd like to share with you the day I woke up. The summer before her last semester in college, Taia had headed off to her Dathun, the month-long meditation retreat way up in the mountains, where there's no cell connection, no checking in, no nothing. Radio silence, from a mother's perspective. Inner Mt. Meru, from the practitioner's perspective. So there I was, no one to battle with, no one to worry about, no one to fixate on; just little me with my life and a whole lot of space in the emotional realm. Big space. After several days of this brand-new spacious experience, whilst doing my own morning meditation, a voice spoke in my head (don't worry, it was me, not a *Voice*), and it said this: *Take your damned credit card back!* I almost fell off my cushion—and I joke not. This sweet solution to the spending problem was so gorgeously simple. And, since Taia was far away, and I wasn't looking into her sparkly eyes, I promised myself I would do just that the second she returned.

The rest, as they say, is history. Within a few hours of her return I called a meeting to retrieve my card (yeah, the one with her name on it—why do credit card companies even offer such a thing?), and she handed it over with a big smile. No argument, no freak-out, just that brilliant understanding that her mother had finally cracked the case. Not that Taia could have articulated it, but, holy moly, was she relieved to be done with that two-way sabotage. Now she could get on with growing up.

Happy to report things have flowed pretty smoothly from there. Our relationship matured almost instantaneously; I was able to get back to being my daughter's true ally, along with re-membering to get on with it, regarding my own life projects and professional pursuits. And, need I even say, I think my work on this riddle has benefited my particular lineage—the grandmoth-ers' spirits are applauding my nice relationship with reality. It's good for everyone, upstream and downstream. Taia's kicking it out in her autonomy, with inspired career aspirations, and our next dog will most certainly be a mutt.

Chapter 36 # Fellowship

The talking stick comes back to me. It hums, as do I, with much appreciation that my better half has told her lyrical mother/daughter story. Notes from the underground that only she could pass along. Amen.

. . . .

I believe we have much to learn from each other. It's also clear for all to see that for Maria and me this guide business is very much a work in a progress, and cuts to the heart of our own personal journey of unfurling, of waking up, and, yes, remembering to have a good laugh about the scrapes and bruises once they have started to heal. So, as mentioned a moment ago, I very much encourage us parents/guides to proceed with a sense of fellowship and generosity toward each other. Let's make it a point to talk. We're all in this together. It's not just about my kids, or your kids, but really it's about nurturing something beautiful and strong in this up and coming generation. Of course, online or via perusing my prior books, you can grab more content about the Types or money-in-marriage or the six areas of personal finance, and that could spur you on to greater things. But, as we all know in this era of digital overload, some of the most powerful gestures in life remain that of human connection, exchange, and—to use a word long since forgotten—the accompanying sense of fellowship. No secret handshakes required, no ring of rings to be deposited in the deep fires of Mordor, just a tenacity of spirit and the willingness to take social risks.

Amble On

As I sit here working at my desk on a glorious June day in Boulder, I acknowledge that *it has come to pass*. No, that is not code for some epic journey awaiting its climax or nadir. Rather, Frodo—I mean, UPS—has just delivered four letters to me, and now I am in possession of $3,000 worth of Phish tickets. In March, the plan to attend the summer run at Madison Square Garden had seemed a brilliant idea. Of course, I didn't anticipate getting every ticket I put in for in the lottery. Nor did I foresee my adventure-appetite shifting so drastically in a mere three months' time, propelling me now to the other coast and a nine-day zen meditation retreat in central California. Yes, I know: My mind has a mind of its own *and* that means in a few moments we'll get to judge the quality of my meditation practice. But first the ticket fiasco.

This morning I spent two hours (that I did not have) unloading tickets on Cash or Trade.org. Tomorrow I will do the same, and then again the day after that. If I'm lucky and good, I'll only lose about $500 when all is said and done. Then I'll have a little sit-down with myself: *Dude, you're a Creative ZM Type. You were*

back in the day. You are now. Tomorrow, if you're living and breath-
ing, you will still be. Therefore, next time, kindly speak to someone
about your "plan" to buy all the 2017 Phish tour ticket inventory. I
know, you and Trey are just about the same age, and you more or
less come from the same part of the world, and you have a friend
from growing up who went to prep school with him—even so, let's
keep your financial knuckleheaded maneuvers to a bare minimum.
To wit, no more freewheeling in isolation. And, yes, no redemp-
tion points forthcoming because the whole family—Taia, Mikyo,
Maria—laughed their arses off at you. Maria was an awfully good
skate about it all ... about your hobbity, bobbity knuckleheadedness.
Do we understand each other?

Um, yes, perfectly.

As I move quickly in my mind to escape further self-lectur-
ing, I land on the subject of enlightenment. Yes, it is so, I was
never much of a believer in *that,* which isn't to say I haven't come
upon a teacher, perhaps two, who really knew how to throw the
juice around the room—*the electric juice*—but that is another
story. As for my own meditation practice, some thirty-five years
down the road of life, I can say this: Some mornings while medi-
tating I remember to breathe properly, perhaps once or twice; or,
I manage to reflect on the people close to me—Maria, and Taia
and Mikyo, and the people they love—and I remember their love
for me, and my love for them. It is so ordinary, but it is also far
too easy to miss, and to project my anxieties and preoccupations
onto those closest to me. I love interrupting *that.* If that is all that
the practice of zazen has led me to, then hot damn, I'm a spiritual
billionaire. For, it's not enough to love and be loved: It's essential
that we know and feel the actual texture of what we've got. Sorry
to preach, but that's what I feel, and needless to say, this corre-
sponds to the inner pulse of this work.

But inner also summons outer. The epic journey is inner *and* outer. The process of individuation doesn't end with me and mine, but rather it extends further out into the social sphere. Diversity simultaneously calls forth social unity and service to each other. We differentiate *and* we merge. Each of us is unique and yet each of us is the earth on which this nation constantly builds itself anew. At least this is what I adore in Whitman's work—this invitation. It is thematic in his life and in his work—in his nurturing the wounded and the dying during the Civil War, his mopping the brow of boys delirious and afraid, writing and reading letters for them to the family they loved, bringing ice cream and writing his friends and family and asking for money for supplies and for nickels and dimes to give the young soldiers, who were really just boys. His poems are a constant political invitation of compassion and care.

The great American bard, Walt Whitman, is inseparable from the enlightened maternal energy of this land. We could rightly say he was a founding grandmother of this great nation, though that might sound too cute. Regardless: His concerns were real. His interest was real. He vetted every nook and cranny of America. He gave a shout out in every direction, to those in the main and those on the margins. He sang the songs of brave individuality *and* he sang songs of unity. Were he alive today, we'd doubtless find him in the hospitals that overflow with the severely wounded of this day. He'd dab the sweaty brow of our kids, irrespective of the party or bias. He'd write letters home on behalf of the wounded, and bring ice cream and treats to them, and solicit nickels and dimes from friends and family and then give whatever he had to them. Why? Because he'd love today's kids. Because in them he'd see millions of suns and know that interdependence—the fundamental truth that everyone is here to play a part, and everyone matters—is the only way through. No poet, no man, has ever loved America as much as Whitman.

I can't not say it one last time:

The young people are the wealth of this great nation, and it is for them that I wave the flag high and wide. Interdependence is stars and stripes. Interdependence is red, white and blue. The call to interdependence is undoubtedly a social call. "Other" is not the enemy. Nor are we the saviors. The modern media primes our minds to weird and destructive biases but I am quite sure we can turn that radio down, if not off, and make other social gestures—gestures way more in keeping with who we really are, fueled by humor and bravery as opposed to being fueled by consumerism and distrust of the "other." It's time for our social awakening. It's time for us to own our micro-aggressions and forgive the micro-aggressions perpetrated by others, and see what's beyond that, because personal independence means little unless, somehow, we come to recognize how deeply we need each other's gifts—no one excluded, not enemies, not people from the heartland or the city or the 'burbs, not crazy people, not purple people. I can hear the whispers of Whitman. *Dear America, it's time to find the divine things enveloped in earth and Nature ... and in each other.* Rocks matter. Bankers matter. Feminists matter. Hair stylists matter. Educators matter. Griots matter. Farmers matter. The homeless matter. The kids matter. And it is on this earthen altar that I leave my prayer. May the kids muster their wisdom, strength, and creative genius to once and for all unite the people of this land, and bring the planetary extremes back into balance. Tall order? Whatever. About the kids and what they can accomplish before the day is done, I have not one doubt.

BIBLIOGRAPHY

Emerson, Ralph Waldo. *The Essential Writings of Ralph Waldo Emerson*. New York: Random House, 2000.

Gilligan, Carol. *In a Different Voice*. Boston: Harvard University Press, 1982.

Goleman, Daniel. *Emotional Intelligence: Why It Can Matter More Than IQ*. New York: Bantam Books, 1995.

Goleman, Daniel. *Social Intelligence: The New Science of Human Relationships*. New York: Bantam Books, 2006.

Hyde, Lewis. *The Gift: Imagination and the Erotic Life of Property* (Chapter 9: *A Draft of Whitman*). New York: Vintage Books, a division of Random House, 1983.

Jay, Meg. *The Defining Decade: Why Your Twenties Matter and How to Make the Most of Them Now*. New York: Twelve (Hatchette Book Group), 2013.

Siegal, Dan. *Brainstorm: The Power and Purpose of the Teenage Brain*. New York: TarcherPerigree, 2014.

Thoreau, Henry David. *Walden; Or, Life in the Woods*. Boston: Ticknor and Fields, 1854.

Trungpa, Chogyam. *Transcending Madness: The Experience of the Six Bardos*. Boulder, Colorado: Shambhala Publications, 1992.

Whitman, Walt. *Leaves of Grass*. New York: W.W. Norton & Co., 1973 edition.

ACKNOWLEDGEMENTS

Debt of gratitude goes to editor *extraordinaire,* Maria Butler. She was pretty much always right with regards to good taste and making sense. Amazing finisher. I can't thank you enough.

Indispensible was the varied and generous council of these good reader folks: Grace Boyle, Carolyn Kanjuro, Caroline Quine, and Mark Washburn. Thank you for your invaluable perspectives and care.

Readers of the opening essay were key in pruning back the early burst of ideas. Thank you to Deborah Krenza, Bill Pearson, Bruce Renfrew, and Michael White.

Susan Wasinger, our talented book designer, was on point in so many ways; most notably, she understood the spirit of *Open Road*, and thus ably translated that into the beautiful visual that you hold in your hands.

Finally, there is the dirt beneath my feet, where I find Walt Whitman. His poetry consistently provided the most nurturing and generative structure for this work. Could not have done it without the great bard. *Merci!*

Open Road is the third of three books on an alternative money universe—a universe that is attuned to self, psyche, spirit, and the earthy side of love and family … as well as money.

As for the author, he's steeped (at the office, at home) in these joyous, provocative, and at times thorny intergenerational moments. Mark's interest in family systems dates back to his years as a family therapist in the late 80s and early 90s.

Boulder, Colorado is home for Mark and his family.